nh

Gila Lustiger was born in Frankfurt in 1963. She studied German and Comparative Literature in Jerusalem before settling in Paris in 1987, where she continues to live and work. She is the author of six published novels and was shortlisted for the German Book prize in 2005. Her most recent novel, *Die Schuld der Anderen* (*The Guilt of Others*), won the Jakob Wasserman Prize. *We Are Not Afraid* (originally published in German under the title *Erschütterung – Über den Terror*) was awarded the Horst Bingel Prize 2016 and the Stefan-Andres-Preis 2017.

WE ARE NOT AFRAID

–

Gila Lustiger

nh Notting Hill Editions

Published in 2017
by Notting Hill Editions Ltd
Widworthy Barton Honiton Devon EX14 9JS

Designed by FLOK Design, Berlin, Germany
Typeset by CB editions, London

Printed and bound
by Memminger MedienCentrum, Memmingen, Germany

A CIP record for this book
is available from the British Library

ISBN 978-1-910749-53-1
www.nottinghilleditions.com

In memory of Marc Dachy

5th November 1952 – 8th October 2015

Contents

– Preface –

In the immediate aftermath of the 13 November, 2015 terrorist attacks on Paris, I sat down, totally devastated, to write this book. I wrote as if driven, day and night for six weeks. I was obsessed with gathering information. I devoured the news on the radio, internet and every newspaper I could find.

I heard about the attacks around 9.30 p.m. as three men in a black Seat Leon were driving through the 10th and 11th arrondissements shooting people out celebrating the start of the weekend on café and restaurant terraces on this unseasonably warm Friday evening in November. I was in a restaurant on the opposite bank of the Seine, listening to the waiter give the specials of the day, when I got a call from my son. He shouted that 'they were driving around shooting at people.' I believed him with no hesitation. In retrospect I am amazed at how unsurprised I was. Since the attacks on *Charlie Hebdo* and Hyper Casher in January 2015 we had all been half expecting a second attack. I realised instantly that he was talking about terrorist attackers. I asked him where he was and whether he was safe and told him not to go out of the house and to put the radio on. I had lived in Israel for five years and in a split second resorted to the old me, living in

1

a country plagued with terrorism and able to react instantaneously. In Paris too it turned out that the radio and social media were the most efficient ways of keeping people in touch and getting information. That same night Facebook set up a page where you could post that you or someone else was safe. And the Twitter account #recplaceparis posted hundreds of photos of missing people, always with the same appeal: If you have seen this person please post. They were often holiday snaps or selfies of happy young people.

The restaurant had a plate glass façade. It would have been all too easy to shoot us. 'We're sitting ducks,' I told my companion. We abandoned our meal. As we were paying, people's smartphones started pinging with the first news, something bad was going down. As yet we had no idea just how bad. I spent that night like many others in Paris. I tried to find out if all my family and friends were safe, absorbing all the information coming from the media on a minute-by-minute basis. On the television, local residents said they had seen tanks, streets cordoned off, soldiers. A radio reporter told of seeing bodies lying in the streets and talked of a hostage situation. We couldn't grasp how many terrorists there actually were: so many attacks were happening at the same time in different places.

President Hollande came on television to announce a state of emergency and that the borders were closed. In the early hours of the morning AFP gave out some figures for the evening and night: more than a hundred people had died and many had been injured in the series of attacks on football fans, on concert-goers, and on customers in cafés and restaurants. Later, the death toll of the Bataclan attacks rose to 130, and the injured to 352. The perpetrators were followers of the so-called Islamic state. Hollande said the attacks had been planned from outside but carried out with help from within. We were all too familiar with the profile of these self-proclaimed holy warriors. It was the same as with the *Charlie Hebdo* and Hyper Casher attackers.

The media soon told us what the police had discovered. They had identified young French and Belgians, aged between twenty and thirty-one, of migrant backgrounds, who had grown up in the suburbs of Paris and Brussels, scraping by with odd jobs, or unemployed. Losers, petty criminals, dropouts, sociopaths. Several had turned their backs on their families. Three of them had gone to Syria in late 2013 and spent months in that country riven with civil war. More than one commentator declared the arrival in Europe of the Syrian generation of terrorism.

We have often been told in recent times that there is no border fence high enough or security measure tough enough to be able to prevent terrorism completely. We're going to have to learn to live with the threat of Islamic violence.

But can you ever learn to live with terrorism? What happens when a café, a concert hall, a train, a shopping mall, a church, a street, a Christmas market, a school –

basically when anywhere we go during the day can be turned into a crime scene at any moment? Of course you can *live* with terrorism. But terrorism is not an inconvenience you just learn to deal with. Terrorist attacks deprive us of our fundamental certainties. Terrorism makes us doubt everything and everyone.

In the days following the attacks many people expressed their outrage and sympathy with the victims by lighting candles, laying flowers, praying, singing, and posting their solidarity with the victims on Twitter or Facebook. Politicians honoured the victims with a minute's silence and called for an unrelenting fight against terrorism.

#prayforparis was followed by #jesuisbruxelles, #prayforistanbul, #jesuisnice, #prayforgermany, for Orlando, for Ansbach, Würzburg, Berlin. People were dying from terrorist attacks in Lahore, Kabul, Kazakhstan, Parachinar, Damascus, al-Arish, Baghdad, Tel Aviv, Maiduguri, Kandahar, Mombasa. Even if we weren't directly affected, we were all aware, if only at the margins of our consciousness, of the images of destruction on the other side of the world.

In her essay 'Observing the Suffering of Others', Susan Sontag explains why sympathy is an unstable emotion. When it cannot be transformed into action, then it withers. She writes that once you get the feeling there's nothing you can do, you become bored.

I don't think I was alone in feeling overwhelmed by all the images of violence, and, saddened, I reacted by withdrawing. The news didn't cause me to think or reflect, but rather to seek solace in my own private world. I wasn't bored by the news, but I did start to push it away, well aware that our democracies were endangered not only by terrorism but also by our failure to come up with clear plausible arguments to counter the voices of populism.

Unsurprisingly, on the day following the attacks, the extreme-right Front National sounded off against the European Union and foreigners, and called for the borders to be closed, and for a referendum on the death penalty. It was this narrative which sought to exclude entire ethnic groups that brought the Front National unprecedented success in the regional elections.

Right-wing populists are not only gaining ground in France. In Holland, Germany and Denmark we see the same phenomenon. How easy life would be if we could stop terrorism by closing the borders. Yet the perpetrators of the 13 November attacks were not foreigners but young people from within our midst. It was French people killing their fellow French. The question was, how was this possible? How could someone who had grown up with one of the most modern welfare states – with accident insurance, old age pensions, sickness benefits, vocational assistance, child, parent and housing benefits, job security, minimum wage and parental leave – come to hate his fellow citizens so much that he would don a suicide vest.

Indeed, what could incite a young man to yearn

so passionately for the 'adventure' of death? And what were terrorism and fear doing to *us*? And when we call for the defence of our values, what, exactly, do we mean: what should we be defending? In order not to drown under the weight of all the news and the helplessness, I had recourse to my bookshelves and the classics. I reread Voltaire and Hannah Arendt, Montesquieu and Kafka, Goethe and Ernst Bloch, Theodore Levitt, Erich Fromm and Marcel Mauss. They gave me the means and wherewithal to confront reality.

In his *Treatise on Tolerance*, Voltaire writes: 'It takes a certain skill to turn people into fanatics and to steer them down that path. But deception and audacity alone are not enough, we have already seen that it's as much a question of coming into the world at the right time.'

What he means by that is that fanaticism can only flourish if the spirit of the times is ripe. Not every era creates jihadists. Ours does.

PART ONE

– France is at War –

In the first days following the Paris attacks of 13 November, 2015, I became obsessed with accumulating information. I read newspapers, listened to the radio, watched countless television reports, trawled the internet looking for announcements and pictures posted under various hashtags, and discussed with friends the updated results of the investigations broadcast to the world by the newsagencies' live feeds; every minute brought new information, it became my life, 24/7.

I did it because I was devastated. Because I wanted to understand what had actually happened, what was about to engulf us, what we had to get to grips with. 'Because "Knowledge is power",' I would reply, quoting the English philosopher Francis Bacon, whenever my family begged to be allowed just once not to wake up to the voices of the *France Culture* or *France Inter* radio journalists. I knew as well as anybody that there was no point in getting bogged down in all this information. I had lived in Israel after all, a country where attacks were daily fare. Over there, psychologists would assert that this sort of information did not actually aid communication, deepen understanding or lead to any conclusion, indeed too much information did nothing to diminish fear – on the contrary it stoked it and rendered people passive. You shouldn't seek out the news for more than an hour a day, unless your life actually depended on it. Instead you should focus on the everyday.

If I had heeded this advice I would doubtless have fed my family and friends better and, to be honest, it would have been more constructive to tidy my office than to obsess about the next alert on my smartphone. Following the attacks my mobile was constantly in my trouser pocket or by me on the table or on my bedside table at night. And always on 'loud'. I even took it with me when I went jogging in the Jardin du Luxembourg, because you could never be too sure. I had become an information junkie and my drug of choice, in this digital age, was instantly available. Unlike José, our local tramp, I didn't even have to go to the supermarket to get my bottle of cheap rotgut. I just had to sit down at my desk and open the browser. I could get my fix with a few clicks of my mouse.

Most announcements came at one remove. 'Our television colleagues tell us,' they would say. Or 'As reported in the newspaper *Libération,* it is possible that' or 'According to eyewitnesses' or '*The Washington Post* reports that'. By the second day the news had already spread around the world. If any of the journalists in the city had come across a single piece of information, a picture or an anecdote, or had even discovered a new eyewitness, or scooped a leaked announcement, then he was immediately quoted by his colleagues. CNN reported what AFP had published, who in turn were quoting *Mediapart* – it was a neverending cycle. Police investigations by their very nature take time, and yet the whole world was desperate for action and results. And above all everybody was needing to be told that something was being done, that measures were being taken that would protect them from what President Hollande on the Elysée Palace Twitter account had called an act of 'absolute barbarism' and an 'act of war'.

'Yesterday's events constitute an act of war,' he wrote, 'in the face of which the country must take appropriate decisions.'

But what were the *appropriate decisions*? The question was debated immediately around the world. From then on I would read analyses by terror experts, psychologists, sociologists, philosophers, social workers, mothers of jihadists, fathers of victims, experts on Islam, Middle East specialists and politicians who were called in to explain to us what had happened and what might yet happen.

Civil society has regretfully become accustomed to the fact that jihadists hate journalists, cartoonists and Jews. But with the 13 November attacks we all became a target. Paris was 'the capital of abomination and perversion' said the so-called Islamic State, when they claimed responsibility for the attacks, and 'this attack was merely the beginning of the storm and a warning for all those who wanted to learn from it.'

The left-wing government learned quickly. The very next day President François Hollande announced a state of emergency. Border controls were introduced, they called up reservists, mobilised soldiers and carried out house searches. On the third day after the attacks, in a speech to the gathered deputies and senators at the palace of Versailles, Hollande announced a whole raft of further measures, including the extension of the state of emergency, a meeting with Presidents Obama and Putin to forge a coalition against IS, the racking up of air strikes on terrorist positions in Iraq and Syria, a reversal of the planned reductions in army personnel numbers, the transfer of the Charles de Gaulle aircraft carrier to Syria and legislative reform which would allow for anyone of dual nationality convicted of terrorism to lose their French passport.

I can clearly remember a brief exchange I had with a friend. We were standing at the bar in one of those bistros where you can pick up your lottery winnings, drinking lemonade and listening to the television above the barkeeper's head.

'France is at war,' started Hollande. 'Friday's attacks are acts of war. We will prolong the state of emergency for another three months . . . but this war, unlike any other we have known, against a new enemy requires a constitutional amendment which will enable us to manage the crisis.'

'What on earth will that mean?' I whispered, horrified, to my friend.

'Give it a rest Gila,' he said. 'I don't want to hear any more!'

I didn't say another word. And when the whole bistro, including the regulars, joined in the Marseillaise with the French MPs and senators, I looked down at my trainers in embarrassment.

Expressions of nationalist feeling scare me. Yet two days later I found myself crying as I watched 70,000 people of both nations singing the French national anthem live from the football international at London's Wembley stadium.

'A shark and an elephant cannot meet and make war. But anything which lives in the same water has, whether it likes it or not, an identity which makes either war or mutual understanding possible,' writes Ernst Bloch in *Farewell to Utopia.* Were we living in the same waters as IS? And who had decided, IS or France? Did President Hollande really have to use the same vocabulary as the very terrorists who wanted nothing other than to foment civil war in Europe? So . . . we were at war. Brilliant, I thought. Had anyone bothered to ask us, the people?

—

I read in an article that the terrorists had opened fire during the sixth song of the Eagles of Death Metal. I knew where the journalist had got his source. In my media obsession I had come across the interview which the drummer's brother had given to WSB-TV in which he reassured the reporter. His brother was fine, he had said, he was at the police station. How weird was that, I thought, that a French journalist based his report on a telephone interview which the brother of an American drummer had given to a small TV station in Atlanta, and then I got to work finding out the title of the song in question. The novelist in me feels that this sort of incidental information should perhaps be looked into a bit more closely to try and establish some sort of meaning.

I spent a morning trawling every conceivable source. In vain. I started ringing around.

'Do you happen to know what song the band in Bataclan played just before the attack? No big deal, it's just I've read the terrorists had opened fire at the start of the sixth song.'

'You and your crazy questions,' was all he said.

My second phone call was equally unsuccessful. 'No idea,' I was told. And 'What does it matter?'

Not until my fourth call did I get the answer I hadn't asked for: 'I know you,' said a friend who really knew me, 'you just want a distraction.'

She was right, of course. And I assume that the journalist too was trying to master his own sense of devastation with concrete facts. The sixth song, that was real – quantifiable. It had clear limits, something happened at the *sixth* song, not the fourth or the fifth, something which none of us understood and which we had to keep returning to ever since 13 November.

What was going on in the heads of those men? What does somebody think about who types, as he did, 'It's starting, we're off' into his mobile, gets out of his car, throws the phone into the nearest bin and goes into a concert venue to shoot into the crowd? What is behind this brutal singularity of purpose? And how can you bring someone to hate so much that he is prepared to turn himself into an instrument of death?

I tried to think myself into his state of quasi-intoxication, into that heady feeling of superiority. He must have felt so powerful as he set off, in the knowledge he was carrying certain death in his bag. And how he must have despised all those who had come, not to die, but to enjoy themselves. According to one of the survivors, he had killed continuously for ten minutes, remaining very calm and composed, only to turn his own body into the ultimate killing machine by blowing himself up once he had fired all his ammunition.

Yet it wasn't just his blind zeal which devastated us, not just the radicality of his actions, not only the realisation that it was possible to kill off all human feeling in oneself. What left us speechless, what we couldn't accept, was that this 'cold fire of the fanatic' – this description is from Erich Fromm, and nothing says it better – this passion without heat had left all of us, victims, bereaved, witnesses, with a sickening feeling of helplessness, of being at the mercy of forces we could not control.

In the days following the attacks we all tried to find words for our devastation and that father who, two days after the bloodbath, still didn't know whether his daughter had survived, spoke the words for all of us. His daughter had moved to Paris from Marcq-en-Baroeul, a medium-sized town with a population of 40,000 to the north of Lille, to work as a lighting technician at Bataclan. Her name was Nathalie, she was thirty-one, and on the picture of her put out on the internet under the hashtag #rechercheparis, which people were using to search for their loved ones, she was smiling and making the Heavy Metal sign, fist raised, index and little finger up, called variously devil's horns or chip fork, depending on where you were coming from.

We had all watched as Nathalie's father spoke to the Prime Minister. Earlier he had been to the military academy in Paris where they had set up a first response station for the families of victims. He had gone through the lists of names, gone to all the hospitals and A&E departments. He had been searching the city for two days and still had found neither his daughter nor any clue as to what had become of her that evening; and now he had decided to play his last trump and buttonhole the Prime Minister Manuel Valls, live on camera. He caught up with him at the Gare du Nord.

'I have no news of my daughter who was in the Bataclan,' he began, and Valls signalled to the security guards to let the man through. 'Nobody can tell me where she is. Why won't anyone tell me anything?' he asked. 'It's unacceptable, unacceptable in this country.'

We had all watched this exchange which lasted all of thirty seconds because it was broadcast on all channels. And we had all seen the shock in the eyes of that father and had realised what he couldn't yet take on board, and each and every one of us could have cried out with him: *This is unacceptable, unacceptable in this country.*

—

The coverage over the last weeks had not lacked for meticulously researched details, which I assume were meant to give us back a sense of reality. Because what exactly do we learn from knowing that the attacker who killed nineteen people and injured nineteen others in the bar *La Belle Equipe* fired a hundred rounds? That he was too wound up to aim properly? That he was a bad shot? Or just really keen? What value is there in knowing that the RAID, the special armed police unit, shot 5,000 rounds in the course of a seven-hour shoot-out in a flat in Seine-Saint-Denis where the terrorists had taken refuge? And what deep insights do we gain from reading that the first attacker in the Stade de France set off his suicide vest at Gate D in the 16th minute of the match?

Undisputed first prize for summing up reality in pithy sentences goes to public prosecutor François

Molins. A journalist writing in the left-leaning news-paper *Libération* even sung his praises in an article called 'I love you Mr Molins' and went on to admit that 'I am not the only one waiting for your press conference. When you appear on the screen, everyone stops talking. Be quiet, Molins is about to speak. We turn up the volume, and, to a man, listen to what you have to say. Imagine, François, a bunch of left-wing journalists hanging on the words of a public prosecutor.' The journalist goes on to say that in a world that has fallen out of kilter, Molins replaced rumour with fact, put a stop to rampant speculation and brought chronological order to chaos.

Since press rooms the world over were hanging on the words of the public prosecutor we now all know that the first attacker triggered his suicide vest at Gate D of the Stade de France at 21.20, the second suicide bomber ten minutes later at 21.30 at Gate H, and the third blew himself up outside a McDonalds at 21.53. That at the same time in the tenth arrondissement at 21.25 an armed attacker shot and killed 15 customers in the bar Le Carillon and the restaurant Le Petit Cambodge and severely injured ten others. And in the rue du Faubourg and the rue de la Fontaine au Roi at 21.32, eleven people died and a further eight were injured. That the attackers killed a further nineteen people in the restaurant La Belle Equipe at 21.36. That at 21.40 a suicide bomber blew himself up and injured several people at the Café Voltaire. And that at 21.40

three terrorists shot into the crowd at the Bataclan concert hall and thereafter two of the attackers, having fired all their ammunition, blew themselves up.

—

'What's this all about?' my son asked me recently in the kitchen as we were standing in front of the fridge eating the day before's leftovers, and waved his fork at a new list on the fridge door.

I love lists, they make me feel secure. They help me to maintain perspective, to divide up my days, to get things done. I often pin lists on my fridge door: shopping lists, notes to self, birthday reminders, appointments, timetables – and this list also had an air of the inventory about it.

'I've decided to write down those pieces of information from the reports on the attacks which I think are beside the point,' I replied and tried to explain to him what had moved me to do it. I talked about the hyperrealism of the reporting, about how we were being bombarded with so much detail that the real issues were invisible. 'It distracts us,' I said. 'It focusses us on details when the big picture, now of all times . . .'

'You don't mean you're going to write a story about the attacks?' he interrupted. He looked at me, horrified.

'No of course not,' I hastened to say. 'Definitely not a story. I'm just collecting again.'

I cut out articles from newspapers, read news

reports and books. That afternoon I had taken Jean Baudrillard down from the bookshelf, along with Erich Fromm, George L Mosse, Voltaire, Richard Sennett and Avishai Margalit. And more books would follow.

'The entrance gates don't belong on here,' said my son once he had perused the whole list and asked me about every single item.

'You mean because they didn't get through?' We called the attackers *they*. We hadn't learned their names. We didn't dignify them with more than a neutral, anonymous *they* when we talked about 13 November because our focus was on the victims.

'And because they're two concrete geographical references.'

He was right of course, writing 'Gate D and Gate H' is not the same as expressing an opinion, or explaining a world view. It's just a statement of fact. *Gate D and Gate H* did not constitute superfluous information. Above all it did not stand for, What would have happened if . . .

Like his two fellows, the attacker who blew himself up outside a McDonald's had tried to get into the stadium where 80,000 football fans were watching the friendly against Germany.

In the queue at the baker's, I'd picked up that the match had been streamed live over TV broadcasts and various internet portals into fifty countries.

'They wanted to create a bloodbath before the eyes

of the whole world,' said a lady who had asked for a particularly well done baguette. And a man standing in front of the cake counter told us that the father and brother of one of the terrorists had been arrested. Another customer opined that the security guards at the gates deserved *La légion d'honneur* just like the four *heroes* who had prevented a bloodbath in the Thalys high-speed train. A fourth commented that Hollande probably had better things to be worrying about. The lady who was paying for her baguette informed us that the area around the Eiffel Tower had been cleared, whereupon another customer pointed out that that it had in fact been a false alarm. And I realised my blood was starting to boil.

The terrorists could not have attracted more attention to themselves if they'd tried, than with a suicide bombing in a stadium during a live transmission. How perfidious, I thought, to commit mass murder during a friendly match; it took some doing to come up with that idea. A massacre during a sporting event between two nations who had been fighting each other for centuries, but who in the aftermath of two world wars had decided to put an end to their emnity. The execution of innocent people celebrating this friendship with football, beer, chips, hotdogs and popcorn. A stroke of media management verging on the genius, if you will. Extremely effective and dirt-cheap to boot. I had read somewhere that a mere thirty-second ad slot during the American Superbowl cost 4.5 million dollars. And what had *they* paid for their gruesome propaganda? Virtually nothing: a bit of explosive, a couple of batteries; the nuts, bolts and screws which they stuffed their vests with in order to increase the death toll – a favoured practice amongst the Palestinian Fedajin – were even easier to come by. And as far as the lives of the attackers themselves were concerned, they were dismissed as mere collateral damage. Yet most of them had grown up in France, I thought angrily. Had had friends here, gone to school here, to sports clubs, had fallen in love here, and perhaps some of their erstwhile classmates had even been amongst the people in the stadium. I forced myself to calm down. Nevertheless there was something here worth thinking through.

By dint of blowing up ancient temples and places of worship, handing over infidel women to its fighters as sex slaves, broadcasting terror videos, beheading its prisoners and now by this brilliantly organised attack in the very heart of one of the world's most respected metropolises, the so-called IS had, in a very short space of time, managed to capture the attention of all media news reporting. IS was manipulating its media image almost as slickly as Coca-Cola, Marlboro, Sony, Nike, Disney or Mercedes. An emigrant from Germany and now Professor at Harvard Business School, Theodore Levitt, writing in the Harvard Business Review, came up with the term *globalisation* which he summarised thus: That the lifestyle and requirements of people in all developed markets were becoming ever more homogenous due to the harmonisation of technical standards and increasingly similar sociodemographic development. Whether consciously or not, IS, like all players on the global stage had clearly internalised this phenomenon. According to Levitt, multinational companies are not the same as global ones. Whereas multinationals adapt their products and marketing strategies to specific countries, a global player, who knows the rules of globalisation and uses them to further his own interests, sticks to doing just the one thing: he sells the same things in the same way everywhere.

But we mustn't allow ourselves to be sidetracked towards the wrong conclusions by all the images and data we are bombarded with: IS and al-Quaida do not 'sell' globalised terrorism, but rather a single ware, namely their backward-looking, fascist world view. But they 'sell it in the same way everywhere' by worldwide terror. We esteem those who propagate this world view 'merely' with words, we deem them to be less dangerous because we wrongly assume them to be part of a religious trend. However, a movement which aims to completely reform state, justice and society according to some religious, 'God given' set of rules and ultimately set up a theocracy which sets no store by our basic rights, such a movement isn't working to a religious agenda but to a political one, and we should fight it with every means available.

Be that as it may, IS (aided by blanket media coverage in the West) is the ultimate threat. Perhaps

21

this partially explains the attraction of this terrorist organisation for so many young people. At the moment it is even overshadowing its competitor in the field of terrorist networks, al-Quaida.

—

There was a great deal of speculation in the world's press about the psychological profile of Hasna aït Boulahcen. It was originally claimed she had blown herself up in front of the anti-terrorist forces in Saint-Denis because, prior to being radicalised and posting 'Soon I'll be in Syria, inch'allah' alongside a picture of herself in a naqib, she had liked drinking vodka and smoking dope, had posed as a rapper and was generally held to be a bit off the wall. The way she was posing for the camera made me terribly sad. I couldn't but think of that other young girl who had moved from Marcq-en-Baroeul to work as a lighting technician in the Bataclan and who had smiled into the camera with a nod to a different music scene but with the same defiant light in her eyes. Now both young women were dead. One a victim of hate, the other having been brought to hatred. I had pondered the pointlessness of these deaths. No word or phrase could ever make sense of them.

There are no words. And yet you can't *not* go on thinking about it. Hasna had dreamed of becoming famous. She would have loved to have seen her photo in the celebrity magazine *Closer* alongside all the stars and starlets, one of her friends told a *Le Monde* reporter. The friend came from Clichy-sous-Bois, 15 kilometres east of Paris, from the very same suburb – and this no passing coincidence – which, following the accidental death of two youngsters in October 2005, saw the start of the youth riots.

PART TWO

– Riots in the Banlieues –

In October 2005, footage of burning dustbins and torched cars focussed the world's attention on France's youth of black African or Maghreb descent – on to their lack of prospects, their bored and resigned lives and their readiness to resort to violence. We learned that faced with youth unemployment and gang criminality they had no chance of achieving upward social mobility.

Quite a few of the attackers of recent years had come from the same 'banlieues' that had gone up in flames. Ismaël Omar Mostefaï, who set off his suicide vest in the Bataclan, came from one of those suburbs, as did Amedy Coulibaly who killed four customers at the kosher supermarket Hyper Cacher on 9th January 2015. Coulibaly had grown up on the Grigny council estate, Mostefaï on a similar estate in Courcouronnes. Likewise Mohamed Merah, who in March 2012 stormed a Jewish school in Toulouse and ran amok shooting dead three pupils and a teacher. He too came from a disadvantaged suburb on the edge of Toulouse. Just like Hasna aït Boulahcen. He had had a different sort of life, a cool life, one involving cars, motorbikes and women; that was before he was radicalised by his older brother. He had the same police record for petty crime as the Kouachi brothers who had grown up in children's homes and fostercare and who on 7 January 2015 carried out the attack on the satirical magazine *Charlie Hebdo*.

And so it goes on, but I want to make what seems to me to be an important point: both Coulibaly and Mohamed Merah, shortly before they killed Jews, had assassinated policemen and soldiers from immigrant backgrounds because they saw them as traitors – as representatives of the state.

In the youth riots back in 2005, policemen and firemen had been attacked and public buildings such as schools, kindergartens, sports halls, post offices, town halls and police stations destroyed. I was struck at the time by the fact that the young people had made no demands. Elsewhere, in my novel *Die Schuld der Anderen* (The Guilt of Others) which appeared early 2015, I addressed this issue thus:

Anyone who thought that these lads had damaged an underground train out of political calculation or torched cars as an anti-consumerist protest had watched too many clichéd Hollywood films. These kids were far too jaded to be under the least illusion that they could change the system. They knew that the best they could hope for was a change of personnel. When they built road blocks it wasn't because they were planning a slave uprising. They left that sort of pretentious nonsense to the erudite sons of the bourgeoisie. What they wanted was to get high on destruction. What they wanted was to get drunk on the display of their own power. They wanted a fix. And they found it anew with each new excess of violence. Their game, for these children of the banlieues, was mindless destruction in its purest, most abstract, most unadulterated form; and what a terribly dangerous game it was. But this generation wasn't protesting against anything, wasn't calling for anything, wasn't seeking anything because they knew for certain, and had always known, that no one gave a toss about them.

Back then during the 2005 youth riots, sociologists like Michel Wieviorka pointed out that there was nobody in the banlieues with whom the state could have negotiated a solution, nobody with the possible exception of the Imams in the mosques. And he sounded a warning that this feeling of having been let down could lead to barbarism. 'Naked violence,' he said in a 2005 interview, 'comes into being in the vacuum created by a lack of any form of communication, morality or ethical values.'

When, precisely two days before the outbreak of the riots in the banlieues, the then Minister for the Interior Nicolas Sarkozy declared that the suburbs needed to be cleaned out with a power hose and called the young people living there scum and riff-raff, he was presumably not motivated by a desire for dialogue. Faced with the reality of the situation three years on, Sarkozy, by then President, promised a Marshall plan for the banlieues. *Espoir Banlieue* as the plan, adopted on 20 June, came to be called, would at last tackle youth unemployment and create equality of opportunity. The policy of zero-tolerance had failed like all the other policies.

According to a recent study by the OnZUS – the national monitoring body for the so-called 'zones urbaines sensibles' – one in five of the French population of immigrant background lives in a tower block estate, characterised by unemployment, petty crime and poverty. In fact 52 per cent of the residents of these estates are immigrants, or children of immigrants who have French citizenship. Most of them come from the Maghreb countries, from Algeria, Morocco and Tunisia – France's former North African colonies. The next largest group is from sub-Saharan Africa or what used to be called black Africa during the time of the colonies. In 2009, 32.4 per cent of people living in the banlieues had to get by on an income below the poverty line. As far as the labour situation was concerned, the OnZUS says that 28.6 per cent of second generation immigrants are unemployed, 52.2 per cent have unskilled jobs. A mere 4.4 per cent of them manage to reach a higher level in the world of employment.

Way back in 2005, social workers, teachers and sociologists were reporting that the banlieuesards also suffered from what they called a 'lack of respect'. Just two years after the riots a high school teacher Emmanuel Renault sent round a questionnaire to twelve banlieue school classes in which he asked them specifically about this issue, which comes up so often in the banlieues. In answer to question 4, as to when in his life he had felt most humiliated, one student in a vocational school in Bondy said: 'in our society today'; another 'on the Champs Elysées'; and a pupil at the vocational school in Argenteuil said it was right to demand respect if, as they all had, 'you had grown up in poverty and had nothing else to defend except your honour.'

It is significant that the 13 November attackers did not carry out their attacks on France's grand streets 'de luxe', where the military strut their stuff on the national holiday. Rather they targeted a popular former working-class quarter, which, as has happened in so many large cities, had become somewhere young sophisticated urbanites go to be seen. The targets of the 9/11 terrorists were New York's World Trade Towers and the Pentagon. The fourth hijacked plane was meant for the Capitol. But the Paris attackers did not choose to target symbols of power. The places they singled out appeared to correspond far more closely to their hatred and feelings of exclusion. Although they declared war on the strong and powerful in their announcement claiming responsibility, it was their own they killed. Quite a few of the victims were successfully integrated, second-generation immigrants.

I came across the following definition of a decent society in the philosopher Avishai Margalit's book *The Politics of Dignity*: 'A society is decent when its institutions do not humiliate people.' A few pages later he defines the term 'humiliation' more precisely:

Humiliation implies an existential threat, because the perpetrator, particularly in the case of an institution, exercises
power over his victim. An essential element of humiliation is
that the perpetrator makes his victim feel totally powerless.

When I read that sentence my thoughts of course
turned to the victims of the 13 November who had
been powerless in the face of their attackers' hatred.

Exclusion and discrimination can lead to terror.
But they don't *have* to. For, even somebody with nothing has something that can never be taken away from
him: the responsibility to decide who he will become.

—

I followed the 2005 youth riots from the reassuring
safety of my middle-class suburb. My children were
still school age. 'What kind of savages are they!' I
thought, as I listened to the radio while getting the
children's breakfast. 'Ignorant fools, destroying precisely that which could enable them to move on.'

Though in fairness, let it be said that the barri-
ers between social classes in France are not exactly
porous. But don't they know that upward social mobility always depends on the education you get? Do they
really have to destroy schools? Kindergartens? Hospitals? One can perhaps appreciate why they would turn
against the police, agents of the state, but why did they
destroy all the emblems of the welfare state? Whenever I heard about a kindergarten set on fire in a Lille

suburb, or a school in the Paris suburb of Sevran, or molotov cocktails being thrown at a hospital in Vitry-sur-Seine, I thought, 'Well then guys, you'd be better off just going back to the village your parents or grandparents came from.' If you don't like living in a country which has had accident insurance since 1898 and unemployment benefit since 1905 go back to your own countries with your African and Arab potentates, civil wars and corruption.

Except that France *was* these young people's own country, young people for whom the French social model was epitomised mainly by the job centre. What's to be done with them? I went on thinking like this for three weeks, as I was fed daily accounts of how many suburbs had been hit, how many cars torched, how many policemen on duty had arrested how many people. Then the riots ebbed away and so did my outrage.

Just a few years later I understood what I had been unable to see before. I had allowed myself to be distracted by the extent of the violence. Every day I had picked up media pictures of the destruction: torched cars, pillaged shops, burning schools, sport halls, bus stops – pictures which the left-wing press used as proof of a failed integration policy and which the political right, amongst others used as proof that it was time to get tougher. Like many women with two small children, indeed like anyone stuck in their daily routine, I think I just didn't listen properly when all the pundits and politicians, sociologists and philosophers, town planners and journalists were explaining on morning radio how, despite a so-called socially integrated urban policy, these uncontrollable riots had been able to happen. Instead I asked my son whether he'd packed his satchel and told my daughter she couldn't wear a summer dress because it was raining.

Ever since the Seventies people had reacted to the cyclical explosions of unrest in the big city suburbs by talking about a *Politique de la Ville* which didn't really seem to mean anything, one way or the other. They set up sports clubs, tore down sprawling estates, launched educational programmes for school drop-outs, started writing and dance workshops, organised town festivals, opened youth information bureaus, held architecture competitions to rebuild the council estates, they laid out green spaces and playgrounds, all this in order to overcome youth violence. This scatter-gun approach reflected the degree to which the politi cal authorities were at a loss to know how to identify and combat the causes behind the collective violence. Anybody active in the social sector of the banlieues could have reported that there was a seemingly limit-less potential for violence dormant there, and that it could be triggered by virtually anything. Yet nobody knew what needed to be done in order to stop these eruptions from happening and who needed to do it, the police or social workers.

Over the years the *Politique de la Ville* had seen

several policy declarations, and every single attempt to get to the root causes of the violence had ended up producing new directives and regulations based on the findings of the latest committee of experts. At the heart of the *Politique de la Ville* were the improvement of both housing and the school system, to mention just two of the policy angles, and both the Marshall plans announced by the politicians of the moment with accompanying media fanfare, had shifted the emphasis towards combatting poverty and exclusion.

Advocates of the first of the policy declarations pointed to the lack of green spaces, squares and places to go, as well the parlous state of the prefab buildings. Repeatedly they called not just for the large estates to be rebuilt but to be torn down. They clearly felt that while the buildings didn't actually produce violence they certainly encouraged it. The wretchedness of these places is obvious to anyone who goes to a cité. A supermarket, two cafés, a newsagent, a take-away, grey buildings, a couple of trees.

Those agitating for school reform asserted that no amount of new building or renovation would do any-thing to tackle youth unemployment, which in some districts topped 50 per cent, and they never tired of talking about the high numbers of school drop-outs in the cités. The kids, they would say, had no hope of getting a job without some sort of school qualification. The banlieue schools were soon being supported with special subsidies which allowed the schools to recruit specially trained teachers and reduce class size. Others tried to tackle unemployment by passing a law, giving tax incentives to companies setting up in the banlieues, whilst yet others tried to deal with the social side of exclusion issues by setting up cultural and sport clubs.

Youth riots have been flaring up at regular intervals in France for decades, always to be followed by public debates about the success or failure of current policy along with new policy declarations and laws. Millions have been poured into the suburbs, and are still flowing, often to the detriment of small provincial towns which are quite simply overlooked. *Le Monde* revealed that in 2008 alone there were a 174 ministerial visits to the problem areas in Seine-Saint-Denis. All the public appearances of members of the government in small towns in the provinces put together wouldn't come remotely close to that kind of media coverage.

The sociologist Dominique Lorrain posited the idea that if you want to be helped by the state these days it's better to be a young, violent, second generation immigrant living on an estate in the banlieues than old and French in a small provincial town letting off steam once every five years by voting for a left- or right-wing extremist party. And he remarked on something so blindingly obvious that I'm ashamed not to have thought of it myself: the folk who participated in the unrest in Vaulx-en-Velin back in 1979 are now nearly fifty and almost certainly no longer hanging round the stairwells of their council flats torching cars. Most likely they've started families, got some sort of job and moved out of the banlieues. Even kids from the suburbs grow up. A sink estate is no Never-never Land. Yet the older folk, the broad swathe of the forty- to sixty-year-olds, they are seldom heard. You only ever see a pensioner from the banlieues on television as the distraught neighbour of some terrorist, live on camera saying how nice and quiet the young man from the second floor had always been.

In his collected essays *The Politics of Poverty*, the sociologist Fabien Jobard, writing about the 2005 riots, observed: 'It's striking that it was not so much the children of the Maghreb rebels of the Nineties who revolted in the Noughties, rather newly arrived immigrants.' He goes on to say that revolt in general is a political experience of disadvantaged urban youth. The urge to violence fades with the passing of youth and gives way to political apathy. But it is wrong to suppose that the idea of youth violence in the suburbs is just an easy cliché. It's not just an idea dreamt up to sell newspapers and stoke up fear. And its very existence, for more than thirty years, just goes to show how powerless the political system has been to improve the lot of those living in the suburbs, despite all the various subsidies and measures. Nothing, not the writing courses, or the workshops or even the cutting-edge design of a green space, not the careers advice in schools (which had actually done little more than traumatise the students), nor yet the billions poured into supporting

34

the labour market, nothing had done anything to lessen the curse of the estates: unemployment.

A 2012 report from the French Court of Auditors sets out the devasting state of affairs in black and white: in 2003 unemployment in the suburbs stood at 17.2 per cent. By 2010 it had risen to 20.9 per cent. In 2006, those living below the poverty line represented 30.5 per cent. By 2008, 32.4 per cent were having to make do with less than 954 euros a month. And the percentage was rising fast.

Would the youth from the estates still have set bins and vehicles on fire if they hadn't been taught at school about the republican principles the French are so proud of that they engrave them above the door of every town hall? Ridiculous and provocative question. Notwithstanding, it is clear that young people in this land of *Liberté, Egalité et Fraternité* feel excluded, and that they have been expressing this feeling through terrifying acts of violence for more than thirty years, generation after generation. As Goethe wrote in the dedication of *Faust:* 'The pain is felt ever anew, the injury remains the same.'

Recently I got someone to explain *Politique de la Ville* to me again. I understood the main thrust of the policy, but was struggling with all the acronyms they used for the laws, decrees and aid measures. The French are obsessed with acronyms, and unless you have a PhD in sociology, they can all too often stand in the way of deeper understanding.

'Go for it,' said my friend on the phone. 'I can give you a quarter of an hour before my next lesson starts.'

'What does ZFU stand for?' I began.

'That's the abbreviation for *Zones Franches Urbaines*,' she said, and explained that companies who set up in the ZFUs were given tax relief.

'Hang on, what is a ZFU exactly?'

'A sort of special economic zone in boroughs with more than 10,000 inhabitants. Boroughs which have a high rate of unemployment but also a high rate of school drop-outs.'

'So you mean the banlieues?'

'No,' she said. 'I don't mean the ZUS.'

'ZUS?'

'*Zones Urbaines Sensibles*,' she said, and that that was a polite way of saying socially fragile residential areas, and that there were currently 751 of them in France.

'So, ZFU zones are within the ZUSs?'

'No, ZFUs are zones within the ZRUs.'

'ZRUs? What are they then?'

'*Zones de Redynamisation Urbaine*,' I was told, and that these 'Zones of Dynamic Urbanisation' were a subcategory of the ZUSs, the ZFUs a subcategory again of the ZRUs.

I could have gone on delving because I still didn't really get the fine distinctions of all the subcategories, but I needed a couple of other acronyms explaining.

'And what are ZEPs?' I asked.

'*Zones d'Education Prioritaire*,' she explained and

added that the schools in these educational priority zones were given more money.

'Do you mean problem schools in problem areas?' I asked, and corrected myself immediately: 'ZEPs in ZUSs?'

'I'm talking about schools where the students fight or insult each other during actual lessons and where they mostly send young teachers who, since they don't have a say in where they go at the outset of their careers, can be dumped anywhere. I'm talking about schools where the teachers stick it out for two years on average, so the staff are constantly changing.'

She knew all too well what she was talking about. The number of ZEP schools had risen constantly over the previous decades. Whilst back at the start of the eighties 350 schools in the suburbs had required special support, the number had grown to 558 by the beginning of the Nineties and to 1189 by the end of the Nineties.

'After that,' she said, 'they reformed the education system. And the ZEP schools were turned into REPs and annexed to REP+ schools in order better to meet the needs of the students.'

'And what on earth does REP stand for?'
'Réseaux d'Education Prioritaire.'

Now I needed to know the difference between an 'Educational Priority Network' and an 'Educational Priority Zone'.

'That's exactly the point people in the FSU were making,' she said.

'FSU?'

'The teachers' union. In 2006 the education system was reformed again, and the ZEP schools were closed.'

'And then?' I asked, because she had stopped speaking.

'And then, nothing. Now the schools are called RARs and RRSs.'

'Okay, so RAR and RRS?'

'*Réseau Ambition Réussite* and *Réseau de Réussite Scolaire*,' she enlightened me, and then after a pause to draw breath: 'You're presumably wondering whether there's any point in calling problem schools "successful striving networks" or "scholastic success networks".'

'Every country has its officialese,' I said weakly.

'That's not officialese,' she retorted, 'it's Newspeak. It's ideological delusionalism.'

And I did indeed remember the term from the novels of George Orwell or Aldous Huxley. She was about to tell me about the ECLAIR schools which had been set up four years later for violent youths, but she had to go to her class and we said goodbye.

It is a mystery to me what was going through the minds of the technocrats who took a failing institution in desperate need of an overhaul and support because its pupil attainment rates were well behind the national average, and renamed it 'Successful Striving Network'. I do actually suspect them of having come up with this new name with absolutely no irony whatsoever, in the genuine belief that it would boost the self-confidence of all those students who up till then had been about to leave school with no qualifications.

They could hardly have made it simpler for themselves. They must have felt so clever: problem sorted overnight, just by making up a new word! Yesterday in 'Educational Priority Zone', today in a 'Successful Striving Network'. Really practical as well, the students didn't even have to leave the area. Because the RARs were in the ZUS, ZRU or ZFU, or whatever these areas were called nowadays. But are these technocrats really so unseeing as to honestly assume that someone living in an HLM – which is the acronym for social housing *Habitation à Loyer Modéré,* an 11-, or 12-, or 16-year-old living with his single working mother and four siblings in a prefab high rise on the outskirts of a big city, would actually be motivated by a name change? Only someone completely ignorant of the day-to-day reality of the youth gangs, who knows nothing of the shadow economy flourishing in the cités, the trade in drugs and weapons, or of the Caids, big and small, these gangbosses who rule over whole neighbourhoods, only someone with this degree of ignorance could possibly believe in all seriousness that a young lad who's doing so badly in school that he needs special assistance, is going to be bothered to find out what RAR even stands for. I suspect he doesn't even know they've changed the name of his school. Network of Successful Striving? Don't make me laugh.

But all this mucking about with names serves only

to illustrate how far removed the technocrats are from reality. More importantly it highlights the fact that social exclusion is necessarily *spatial* exclusion. The Marshall plan which the French state drew up in 1996 for the banlieues just left the poor where they were. The ZUSs, ZFUs and ZRUs are in very clearly demarcated areas where poor people live separated from the rest of society. The wealthy segregate themselves. They stay, with others of their ilk, in their chic resort hotels, in their posh neighbourhoods, in their expensive restaurants.

—

The original immigrants from north and black Africa who worked in the factories and returned home tired after a long day had nothing against the flats in the dormitory towns outside the big cities not far from the industrial estates that had been built for them between 1950 and 1974. Their French-born children and grandchildren, however, who have had to grapple with lack of prospects and joblessness clearly do have a problem with them. Had the majority of jobs not been lost in the shift from a manufacturing economy to a service based society, perhaps these bleak places would somehow still be fulfilling their purpose. The estates were built for workers not for the jobless.

A year before the unrest started in 2005 the PRU programme (*Programme de Rénovation Urbaine*) had poured 650 million euros into Clichy-sous-Bois, a borough 15 kilometres east of Paris with 30,000 inhabitants. A thousand new homes were built, 700 old ones demolished with the aim of encouraging those families who wanted to move up into the lower middle class to stay in the town. Yet many still move out as soon as they can afford to, because nothing has really changed. The council remains the largest single employer, with 400 jobs, followed by the hospital and the E.Leclerc supermarket.

There have been poor neighbourhoods since time immemorial. People have been angry at being excluded since forever too. In previous centuries they dealt with the problem of the poor simply by sending them away; thus, apart from a few daredevil adventurers, it was the excluded, the dispensable, the superfluous who conquered new territories and built empires for Europe. But now there is nowhere left to conquer, empires have risen only to fall again. Clichy-sous-Bois has 30,000 residents, including many from the former French colonies. Where do you send people today who know what being superfluous in our societies feels like? What do you do with people who, economically speaking, have become worthless and who are fed up with living in jerrybuilt housing blocks and having to make do with handouts from a welfare state?

In his benchmark publication *Die Gabe* (The Gift), Marcel Mauss writes that in ancient societies it was compulsory to reciprocate a gift with another. Self-esteem and the respect of others were accorded only to those who could give something back in return, no matter how small. According to Mauss:

It took the triumph of rationalism and mercantilism to give any credence to the concepts of profit and the individual and even to allow them to be raised to the status of principles.

. . . [In Maori law] a bond created through an object is a bonding of souls . . . Accepting something from another was tantamount to accepting a part of his being, a part of his soul.

It strikes me that the gestures of giving, taking and reciprocating, still stand as bulwarks of social bonds. A welfare state, with its aid programmes and funding packages, only gives. Richard Sennett in *Respect in an Age of Inequality* makes the point that: 'When we do not expect anything back, we are sending a clear signal that we do not perceive the relationship between us and the recipient of what we are giving as one based on mutuality.'

Respect can only exist in the presence of reci-procity.

Like all my 'leftie' friends in the autumn of 2005, I condemned the conservative government for cutting funding for neighbourhood policing and subsidies for clubs and groups in the cultural sector. Yet in moments of honesty, I had to admit to myself that a writing workshop and a hip-hop course wouldn't in all probability change very much. Though doubtless

noble-minded to want to help young people sublim-
inate their frustration through creativity, might it not
have been more helpful to find out why they were frustrated in the first place? But why *were* they frustrated?
Could the causes behind the unrest really be reduced
to its social dimension?

I had to see things for myself in order to work out
what it was I hadn't been told or what, quite simply, I
hadn't been capable of reading or hearing. So I set out
to see the terrain for myself. Truth to tell, however much
I had discussed the situation in the banlieues with my
friends, there was not a single one of us whose daily
lives had really been affected by the riots unfolding
way out beyond the city limits. Personally all I knew of
Paris' banlieues was Bobigny because the guest directors at the MC93 Theatre brought in actors like Peter
Sellars, Bob Wilson, Deborah Warner, Peter Zadek,
Klaus Michael Grüber and Lev Dodin. In the queue
for drinks and sandwiches in the interval I would meet
at least four or five people I knew, who like most of the
other theatregoers, had driven out from Paris in their
little cars which they had left safely in the guarded car
park and which they would be driving straight back in
again as fast as they could after the performance.

PART THREE

– Us and Them –

In March 2012 Mohamed Merah killed three children and a teacher at a Jewish school. I had already started sitting up and paying attention before then. More and more of my Jewish acquaintances were telling of encroaching anti-semitism, orthodox Jews being molested or beaten up, Jewish businesses and synagogues sprayed with hate-filled insults or even set on fire, Jewish children in the banlieues state schools being bullied and moved in droves to the private sector. As yet the media hadn't become aware of this new anti-semitism, but it was putting down roots – springing not as it usually did from the extreme right camp but from the banlieues. All the attacks were perpetrated by young Muslims and the victims were Jews who didn't have the privilege I had of living in a nice middle-class neighbourhood. My Jewish friends wondered where this was all leading. And wondered whether they would even want to go on living in France.

I tried to explain away my unease by linking the anti-semitism in the banlieues to the conflict in the Middle East. In truth anti-semitic attacks had been on the increase year on year since the second intifada and flared up whenever war or unrest broke out some 3,000 km away from Paris. Not infrequently, shows of solidarity with the Palestinians would take the form of calls for violence against Israel and Jews, for sooner or later cries of 'Jews out!' or 'Death to Jews!' would rise up through the mob.

'*Mort aux Juifs!*' – That's what they had shouted in France during the Dreyfus affair, and what they had practiced under the occupation. Nevertheless after the war, we Jews had believed we would never again be victims of hate in Europe. And now this: the banlieuesards had unambiguously joined cause with the Palestinians in Gaza. And yet, even after several hundred demonstrators armed with sticks and baseball bats had attacked a synagogue in Rue des Tournelles in 2014, I did wonder whether this identifying with their 'brothers' in the Middle East wasn't just a welcome excuse.

At the time I was standing in a bar not far from the synagogue together with other football fans watching the broadcast of the World Cup match between Germany and Argentina from the Maracana stadium in Rio de Janeiro, completely ignorant of the masked mob moving on from the synagogue in the Rue des Tournelles to the next one in Rue de la Roquette. I only heard about it the next day. The news had spread like wildfire amongst my Jewish friends. The Merah affair was forgotten, Hyper Cacher and *Charlie Hebdo* were yet to come. The next day the papers were mainly talking about how Mario Götze had snuck into the penalty area, taken the ball from Schürrle on his chest and kicked it straight past the Argentinian keeper into the goal with his left foot.

I dropped by an old friend's who had survived the camps – actually she never talked of herself as a 'survivor', rather as a 'returnee' – and obviously she didn't want to talk about Götze's goal. We sat in her kitchen drinking pomegranate juice, which she had delivered from an Armenian shopkeeper, and eating gugelhupf, when she confessed that she couldn't help but think of Kristallnacht.

'It's just a few rioters.'

I tried to distract her. It's not driven by the state. History's not repeating itself. Nobody's building any camps. She wasn't being forced to wear a star. But I admitted to myself that I was dismissing her fears too lightly. Not that I was tired of her fears as such, but of talking about anti-semitism altogether. Just recently I had declared an evening to be 'an anti-semitism free zone' as she had started telling me about the conspiracy theories doing the rounds on the internet that World Jewry / the Zionists / the Jewish lobby in America / the media / the financial markets . . . were ruling France.

'We're not going to talk about what they're saying, nor what they're thinking and definitely not what these arseholes from the cités are doing to us now.' I had been shocked by my own vehemence and had apologised. I craved to be like everybody else just for once. I'd like to chat about the 113th minute of the match. Football rather than anti-semitism. How come anti-semitism is only ever something Jews talk about? Isn't it enough that of late we have been beaten up, raped, tortured and even killed? Do we really have to discuss it in our homes? And why on earth did I feel morally obliged to write about it? Because the general public doesn't take any notice of anti-semitic attacks?

French Home Office statistics show that just under half of all attacks classified as racist were carried out against Jews – bearing in mind that Jews make up less than one per cent of the population. Other people can grapple with this this evening. We'll hand the subject over to them to deal with. In a couple of hours we'll order Gyoza, your favourite dumplings filled with meat, leeks and ginger, from the Japanese restaurant round the corner, drink an ice-cold Japanese beer and watch the goal in extra time which won Germany the world championship on YouTube.

Except – where were those others? And why were they so little interested in the fact that synagogues were being desecrated? What upset my friend was the indifference to the fate of the Jews – the same ubiquitous, smiling indifference which had allowed my friend as a young girl to be deported to Drancy assembly camp and thence to Auschwitz-Birkenau. And I had no argument, could come up with no proof to convince her that, throughout this rainy summer, this new, savage hatred of the Jews devastated anyone but ourselves, the Jews.

The steadily rising number of anti-semitic attacks was not the only sign of upheaval in France, the social unrest told the same story, and I resolved to take a closer look at the country. A friend's niece, a police-woman in the drug squad, got me into the criminal investigation department. For several weeks I immersed myself in the world of drug dealers, drug addicts, murderers, victims, witnesses and petty criminals, prostitutes, pimps and punters.

Once, after a day spent surrounded by wretchedness – criminals not even twenty years old, with police records like fifty-year-olds having lived through all possible variations of social marginalisation, brutalisation and violence – I missed the métro stop where I should have changed trains. I decided just to stay on the train. At some point I got out. It was a warm autumn evening. Lost in thought, I walked along the Seine which was reflecting the last of the sunrays, and went on to Place de la Concorde, crossed the rue Royale, almost empty at this hour, past the five-star hotels. I probably needed the magnificent façades, the broad streets, the pomp and circumstance, and I imagined the tourists in their rooms. Imagined them getting ready to go out to a concert or a restaurant. In my mind's eye I saw women putting on their make-up, their husbands in their socks reading the newspaper on the bed. I saw chefs explaining the menu to waiters, chambermaids changing towels, the whole invisible workings of a Grand Hotel; all at once I realised I had wandered down as far as the rue St Honoré, that shopping street with all the luxury boutiques not far from the Elysée palace. I looked in the shop windows. In most of them there was only one, maybe two, articles on display. They had been so artfully displayed that they actually told stories.

I don't have anything against luxury goods, especially not in a country like France, where ever since the reign of the Sun King, luxury has been not only an expression of the status of its owner but also, importantly, a sign of opulence, of finesse and pleasure. Here luxury still harks back somewhat to its Latin origins, because it is indeed a contortion, a dislocation, always extravagant, not solid, careful precision work, but excessive and wasteful. No, I have nothing against luxury, rather against mass produced goods, made in dangerously ramshackle textile factories in Bangladesh, against child labour in Chinese toy companies, against all inhuman working conditions in those countries where the rags we wear for a season get sewn. In an age where one in three people work in the service sector, a branch which provides work for bespoke shoe makers, seamstresses, goldsmiths, saddlers, silk-engravers and handbag-makers almost feels like a relic from a bygone era. And as I leant forward to read the price on the tiny black label on a satchel-sized calfskin handbag, I didn't get angry because of the price, but I did wonder whether anyone who was prepared to pay 7,500 euros for the thing was capable of imagining the daily life of someone who has so little that he must go without everything which makes for a comfortable life in today's society.

Is it necessary that rich people know how it feels to be poor? Did it matter whether someone who was living on the edge of poverty, knew of the existence of bags which were made by hand exclusively to order and for which you had to be on a waiting list? Rich folks' waiting lists are not for council flats, but for handbags. If social cohesion relies on shared loyalties, do we need to be able to imagine the lives of those we almost never see?

I was distracted from my train of thought by a scene playing out on the opposite pavement where a couple were arguing. The scene as such was fairly run-of-the-mill, and yet I watched them in amazement along with all the other passers-by. It was not the fact that they were arguing which so surprised us, but more that they were doing it in the middle of the street, and very noisily at that. At some point the couple disappeared into a car and the people started moving again. I too set off for home.

As I was strolling past the shops where the last customers were leaving, I realised all of a sudden that this neighbourhood had until now been spared any crowd violence. Obviously all sorts of dramas played themselves out behind the facades of the villas and mansions, here like everywhere else, but the so-called blind rage of the people which so regularly boiled up in the suburbs had never spilled over into these bourgeois streets which bordered the neighbourhoods where Power dwelt. The political, financial and cultural elites lived in Paris, but the rebellion by the disempowered took place not far away, yet far enough from the city centre, at a safe distance in the suburbs. I went home to check out my suspicions.

And there it was: in the course of the youth riots in 2005 which began in Clichy-sous-Bois near Paris and spread to 300 suburbs and all over the country, gangs of youths torched 10,000 cars and 230 schools, kindergartens, libraries, town halls and police stations were destroyed. 11,200 members of the security services were called into action, nearly 3,000 people were arrested and 126 police injured. The riots lasted three weeks and caused damage to property to the tune of 200 million euros and at their zenith triggered a state of emergency, but none of the young people stood on the barricades in Paris. The youths destroyed anything, even a bus-stop, remotely connected to the state, but the state itself, its institutions and representative bodies remained unscathed.

Every year on the 14 July, the French commemorate the 1789 storming of the Bastille. They have made the date into their national day. The country's history is present everywhere. The nation is proud of its revolutionary past, the Paris Sans culottes uprising, the abolition of feudalism, serfdom, the fiscal privileges of the nobility and the clerics, slavery in the colonies. So why in a country like this did it not once occur to any of the rioters to follow any of the oft-cited examples of the past? How come they never stormed the Bastille?

The reporters of the time wrote often of wild, unchecked violence. But however unrestrained the riots may have appeared to eyewitnesses, the youths only rioted in their own cités. The single most staggering aspect of the riots, when you actually thought it through, was how modest the young had been in their fury, how limited in their thinking. Clichy-sous-Bois lay a mere 15 kilometres, as the crow flies, from Paris; about three quarters of an hour by car in normal traffic, perhaps a bit longer on public transport. And yet it did not occur to any of them to barricade the streets of Paris, stop the traffic and demonstrate in front of the National Assembly or the Elysée Palace, unlike all the other strikers and malcontents over the years . . . farmers from Brittany, taxi drivers, nurses, doctors, teachers, craftsmen, barristers, solicitors, chemists, opticians. These rioters were rebelling against exclusion but had remained the whole time within the boundaries of their neighbourhoods. It's not as if there were even any fences! Nonsense, of course there were – fences in their heads.

It never came to class war during the youth riots. Not even to a clearly articulated protest. For that the rioters would not only have had to stand before the institutions or their representatives, but also to have made clear demands. But they had no spokesmen. And they had no aim. The rioters were not social revolutionaries either – and yet the damage to property, the arson and even the looting can only be interpreted as a protest against prevailing conditions. The disastrous thing about these riots was that the mob had no voice. If there are demands there can be discussions. Demands, even when made with violence, can be integrated into a democratic political process. But what can you do with rioters who make no demands?

Poverty, joblessness, feeling excluded do not necessarily lead to violence. And even back in 2005 nobody was able to say definitively which factors, what confluence of events had led to the youth of the suburbs getting high on their own violence for three weeks.

For sure, the fact that it was a holiday period did nothing to help the situation. Many opinion makers declared the Republicans' integration model dead and buried, and called for American-style affirmative action. The affirmative actions which came into being in Sixties America, policies designed to favour members of disadvantaged groups, were intended to open up access to employment and institutions of learning to members of minorities, by introducing quotas, amongst other measures. Recently I came across an oft-quoted passage from President Lyndon B. Johnson's speech made in June 1965, at the historically black Howard University, where he set out the principles of affirmative action:

You do not take a person who, for years, has been hobbled by chains and liberate him, bring him up to the starting line of a race and then say, 'you are free to compete with all the others,' and still justly believe that you have been completely fair.'

However, it is difficult to implement measures like this in France because it is illegal to classify people on the basis of origin, ethnicity or religion. France is a society of equals, and the extent of the violence can safely be read as a clear sign that the second generation immigrants had internalised the republican values of equality and brotherhood and were confronted daily by the discrepancy between theory and practice.

The pundits were already making comparisons with Ramallah. Pictures of youths throwing stones made such comparisons easy. On the tenth day of the riots the UOIF (*Union des Organisations Islamiques de France*) issued a fatwa to stem the unrest and more and more Islamic organisations came forward as keepers of order and positioned themselves between the police and the rioters, and as ever the far-right Front National stoked up fears of the Islamisation of France, so those self-identifying as bourgeois hardly even posed the question as to whether the motivation behind the up-risings was religious or ethnic in nature, or whether they could be manipulated to further religious or ethnic agendas. And yet several social workers did point to the danger of an ethnicisation of social conflict.

Indeed Islam did play an important role in the self image of these young people, even though it was not what had actually driven them on to the streets. Those Muslims in particular who had integrated into French civil society were angered by the fatwa, whilst recognising that any religious counter culture positioning itself as an alternative to state authority bore within itself the germ of its very exclusion from French society. People of many different affinities noted with concern the number of mediators coming from Islamic groups. Home Secretary Nicolas Sarkozy for one was in no doubt that the youth of the banlieues were subject to French law and not to the moral principles of a religion, but that hadn't stopped him from suggesting the idea of the fatwa to the UOIF with a view to minimising the influence of radical Islamists and getting the riots under control. That earned him the sobriquet 'the great Mufti' from his opponents for several weeks after.

At the time all the commentators were wondering whether such outbreaks of violence could happen again. But presumably not even the most dyed-in-the-wool pessimists among them could have supposed that ten years on a twenty-nine-year-old Frenchman of Algerian origin from the Paris suburb of Courcouronnes, along with a twenty-eight-year-old bus driver from the Paris suburb of Drancy and a twenty-three-year-old jihadist from Strasburg would blow themselves up in a concert hall in Paris.

———

In the course of the 2005 youth riots, thirty-two libraries were burnt down or so badly ravaged that their contents had to be thrown away. If one looks at the period covering 1996 to 2013 the tally rises to more than seventy. Libraries come under attack in the banlieues again and again. An attack can vary from broken windows and graffittied walls, via broken or looted furnishings and riots in the reading rooms to intimidation of the library staff. At the time the situation in the banlieues was giving rise to other, more pressing, causes for concern and not much attention was paid to this phenomenon.

Why did a place that not even ten per cent of the local residents used attract the wrath of the rioters to such an extent? What led them to desecrate and destroy this source of culture which was made available for free? Libraries are set up by the organs of state to raise social standards. So what do you do then when the very people for whom they were set up, not only reject them but actually destroy them?

The sociologist Denis Merklen stands alone in his search for an answer to this issue. In a case study published in 2014 and entitled simply *Why do they burn libraries?* he attempts to get to the bottom of what exactly it was that the rioters were attacking when they demolished yet another library. Between 2006 and 2011 Merklen interviewed many of those who had participated in those dramatic events in the département Seine-Saint-Denis, known colloquially as 'neuf-trois' from its postcode reference 93, and home to several of the social flashpoints such as Clichy-sous-Bois, which took place, like all the other signs of youth radicalisation, on the outer reaches of public awareness.

Merklen's conclusions make clear that the educational model motivating the builders of the libraries utterly failed to relate to the young of the département for whom all this unstinting largesse was being spent. In Clamart they even furnished the library with designer furniture from Alvar Aalto, Arne Jacobsen and Harry Bertoia, which is now worth a fortune at auction. Whilst for some, libraries represent one of the cornerstones of a democracratic society, guarantors of knowledge and culture, forgers of enlightend opinion and ambition, for others they constitute nothing less than yet further humiliation. Many of the rioters were school drop-outs and their hatred was directed not just towards books but towards the written word in general which they saw as an instrument of their subjugation. Far from offering a way out of their milieu for these young people, the realms of language and the written word stood for only one thing: bureaucracy. Language skills were essentially for filling out the official forms they needed at the job centre or benefits office to get a medical slip or a certificate to obtain their dole money. Language meant laws telling them what they could and couldn't do. Just another way of fencing them in. Teachers, social workers and police laid down the law from outside; from inside, it was Language which kept them down: 'They build us libraries to anaesthetise us. So we sit reading nice and quietly in our corner. We want jobs, and their answer is "Get an education and keep quiet",' one of Merklen's interviewees said.

If that young man had left his comfort zone and done something really daring, set off on a journey into the unknown, had he, in other words, opened a book, he would have seen that somebody before him had made precisely the same demands of the lords and masters who are all too keen to teach you how to 'live in obedience and avoid sin and misdeeds'. As Brecht's Macbeth in *The Threepenny Opera* sings: 'You may proclaim, good sirs, your fine philosophy/But till you feed us, right and wrong can wait. Or is it only those who have the money/Can enter in the land of milk and honey?'

But how does one communicate with people who see their own language as the enemy? How can one reach them if not through education and culture? Here I'd like to relate an incident from my own life: My children went to a state kindergarten just round the corner from our street which was affiliated with a primary school. When my eldest started school, some twenty years ago now, we were summoned to the headmistress. Anxiously we turned up for the meeting. Once we had sat down I was asked about my life up to that point. The headmistress had picked up on how I spoke German with my son, also he had boasted to the teacher that he had an Israeli Grandma and an aunt in London. What's the problem with that? I asked. Nothing, the headmistress hastened to reply – she must have felt that I was about to cast her as an anti-semite – just that she would ask me to speak only French with my son in the first two years of primary to make it easier for him to learn the written language. We thanked her and went to a café to confer.

'Are you prepared to speak only French to them for two years?'

And I thought about *Pumuckl, Jim Knopf, Die kleine Raupe Nimmersatt, Das kleine Ich bin ich*, about *O wie schön ist Panama, Eine Geburtstagstorte für die Katze, Das doppelte Lottchen, Das kleine Gespenst* – about all those books I'd have to read in French translation to my children, and I said I couldn't possibly do it.

'Then they'll just not turn into fully paid up French citizens,' I said and added that I couldn't give up my mother tongue. Within the month we had found a private school for the children, which did not object to foreign languages.

Three years later, when my daughter started school, I had a problem which I stumbled upon on by chance one evening towards the end of her first year at school when my daughter read aloud a short passage from her reader.

'We've got a bit of a problem with our daughter,' I told her father later.

'Aha, what problem?'

'She's not reading, she's learning the words off by heart.'

'Nonsense,' he retorted and asked our daughter to bring her book into the lounge with us. 'Sweetheart,' he said. 'Can you just read aloud to Mummy what you read me yesterday?'

'The story with the giraffe?' asked our little girl.

'Exactly,' he said looking reproachfully at me.

She sat down, found the relevant passage and read the text fluently and faultlessly. I finally caught her out on the fifth or sixth word I pointed to. I pointed to *Haus* but she had miscounted and said *Giraffe*.

'So,' I asked. 'Believe me now?'

Through friends we found a tutor. One time when I asked her to join me for a glass of wine, we started chatting and she told me she taught in a ZEP school and was against private schools, against the creation of elites and actually against tutoring in richer neighbourhoods.

'I agree with you completely in principle,' I said. 'But when it's your own children you make an exception, don't you?'

I told her what the headmistress at the state school in our street had demanded.

'If your child was at my school you wouldn't feel like a foreigner.' There were children from fifteen different cultures in her class alone, she went on, who, as far as the buzz words *flexibility* and *mobility* were concerned would have coped easily with any kid from the cadre class! 'But then you probably wouldn't have sent your son to Clichy-sous-Bois would you?'

I laughed. 'To Clichy-sous-Bois? Honestly? No.'

'Because you associate it with unemployment and youth crime?'

'Amongst other things,' I said, 'and also the large number of school drop-outs.'

'Did you know that the people who live there come from ninety different countries?'

I hadn't known that.

'Clichy-sous-Bois is a little world unto itself,' she said.

'It's just that my son wouldn't really . . .'

She interrupted me. 'These kids may have problems with French grammar but they know the customs and rituals from at least ten other countries. They know that the traditional singers of the Malinké are called Dweli and their stringed instrument is a Kora. And they know that 250 ethnic groups live in the Congo and speak more than 200 separate languages. And that "Burkina Faso" means "Land of the honourable", and that at births, weddings and funerals in the Gabon they wear masks.'

She talked for a good hour about the children. I listened and tried to imagine the life of this young woman, who was always perfectly turned out when she came to us. I imagined her getting up at six, showering and putting on her make-up in her little bathroom. Then she would have a quick breakfast standing up and hope she wouldn't get stuck in traffic. Then she would take the RN3 over the Porte de Pantin towards Meaux, or the A3 over the Porte de Bagnolet, the exit for Bondy. Then she would drive past the graffiti-covered sound insulation walls, to the place that everyone else was trying to flee. And then finally she would get out of her second hand Renault Clio and cross the carpark in her flat-heeled shoes. Yes, I thought, she's one of the extraordinary people who don't define the kids by their weaknesses. Did that mean they suffered less from so-called socio-psychological difficulties, or faced fewer developmental challenges? Hardly. And yet every day this young woman got up and went to teach *her* children how to read and write, despite all the difficulties and the doubts which she must surely have had to deal with.

'You love them, don't you?'

She looked at me surprised.

'The children,' I said. 'You love them.'

'What makes you say that?'

'You only have to open a newspaper and read what's happening in Clichy-sous-Bois . . .'

'So you think I romanticise them,' she interrupted. 'What if I do? Would that be so terrible? Doesn't everyone need a bit of spontaneous sympathy?'

I nodded, and we finished our wine in silence, then she looked at the time and said she had to hurry, so I showed her out.

The next Monday I got home a bit later than usual. My daughter gave me a note from her tutor. On a page of squared paper, in her open, rounded writing stood: *Do we not all blossom under the gaze of someone who recognises what we are capable of?*

—

How come hardly anyone really noticed that libraries were being destroyed and librarians attacked?
How come it didn't bother any of us? That images of
burning books didn't frighten us? That not even I was
reminded of the 10 May 1933? That those sadly all too
familiar images did not superimpose themselves in
my mind's eye on to the images of libraries burning in
the suburbs? Why weren't all my alarm bells ringing?
Why didn't I remember Joseph Roth's prophetic words
to his friends before the takeover of power in Berlin,
1932: 'They will burn our books, but in their hearts it
is us they burn.'

Seventy libraries in flames, and not one of us
gave much consideration to the consequences of this
encroaching phenomenon. It occurred to no one to
recognise in these attacks symptoms of a disease whose
natural course was to culminate in the assault on *Charlie
Hebdo* and the terrorist attacks of the 13 November.
Why did nobody point out that when they start burning books, soon they turn on the authors? The only
possible answer is that none of us took the rioters from
the banlieues seriously until the day when a dope-
smoking pizza delivery boy and his–brother stormed
into the editorial offices of a magazine in order to kill
twelve people. With the same blinkered condescension
that the German chattering classes deigned to notice
the noisy SA rabble back in the day, we paid brief attention to these losers, benefit scroungers and school
drop-outs who were down in the suburbs torching the

cultural heritage we had so graciously made available to them that they might usefully better themselves. We were dismayed, maybe somewhat disappointed, shocked, confused because they were destroying our culture. But were we frightened of these Philistines? Not in the least.

People have been burning books ever since there have been books to burn. Those doing the burning had different motives. They burnt books they judged to be heretical or obscene, blasphemous or inflammatory, decadent or hurtful, but despite their differences of doctrine they all fell back on the same explanation: they divided the world into friend and foe, us and them, more and less valuable, into good and bad. The library arsonists in the banlieues acted with no ideological framework. And for precisely that reason: just because they didn't shout fire and brimstone invective when they threw the books, we forgot that the rage which leads a person to burn down a library contains the germ of the same idea: the rioters too were dividing the world into Us and Them.

We assumed that with the libraries they were destroying symbols of the state and many of us tried to justify this cultural vandalism by looking at social dysfunction and the frustration it engendered. But we forgot that anyone who is so suspicious of culture that they destroy it (all fascists incidentally), will sooner or later lose the capacity to think critically – the very capacity which makes discussing differences of opinion tolerable, even desirable. For culture and literature invite one to see the world through the eyes of someone else. And a library is always going to be one of those spaces which allow ideas, religions, worlds, sensibilities, experiences and opinions to co-exist and flourish.

It is all too easy to equate a book with its author, or confuse an author with his work, as the words of one of the Kouachi brothers show so clearly. The scene was filmed on a smartphone by a witness who had managed to escape onto a roof and it was doing the rounds on the internet the next day. As the brothers were running back to their black Citroën C3 one of them cried out: 'We have avenged the prophet! We have killed Charlie Hebdo!' He could have named the cartoonists, or called out their *noms de plume*, because in the final analysis, they hadn't shot Charlie, but Charb, Cabu, Tignous and others, but for that they would have had to have seen their victims as individuals. They had been indoctrinated by an ideology which dehumanised and demonised others.

What can you possibly say to someone who claims he would rather obey God than Man and thus is convinced that he will go to heaven if he cuts your throat? More often than not the fanatics are guided by villains, who press the dagger into their hands. – Voltaire, *Treatise on Tolerance*.

After the *Charlie Hebdo* attack this plea for tolerance,

which first appeared in 1703, reached the bestseller list, because many French people affirmed their values through the medium of culture. It's a paperback and costs 2 euros. Needless to say, this brief text, in which Voltaire sets out the need for tolerance, would have been on loan from one of the destroyed libraries.

We must all bear with one another, because we are all weak and faltering, we are all subject to change and error. Does a reed who is bent down to the mud by the wind say to another reed which is bent in the other direction: Bend the same way as me or I will complain and get you pulled up or burnt?

The attacks which the media paid attention to at the time were assaults on children and teachers. Unlike in Germany children in France are at school all day. Even kindergartens go till 5 p.m. which allows many women to go out to work. So school is where a French child spends the greater part of his day. It is where he is socialised and learns to integrate into society. Not for nothing is the ministry of education called 'éducation nationale'. Ever since the introduction of the Jules Ferry education bills in 1881 and 1882 which oblige the state to give boys and girls a free and secular education, children here are brought up to be French citizens. The basic principles underpinning the French education system are equality and secularity (and it's free of charge). So news items about the destruction of schools hit the French hard.

When the socialist minister of education Vincent Peillon was confronted on his first day in office with the reality of increasing violence against teachers from their pupils, he spoke in the media of a moral decline amongst students and created a post of 'Delegate for the prevention of and combat against violence'.

Over and over again in recent years there have been reports about the atrocious conditions in French educational establishments which inevitably end with a polemic over 'refusal to integrate' or 'parallel societies', whether the schools in question were in the banlieues or not. I remember reading in *Figaro* that in the school year 2012/13, 1500 teachers had reported being physically assaulted. And I vividly recall the brief exchange I had with an acquaintance. The journalist in the right-wing daily had got access to the database of the teachers' insurance organisation, MAIF. I assume, as is often the case with such revelations, that an employee of the insurance company had tipped her off. Thus we learnt that 23,000 teachers had demanded legal advice from their insurers because they had been threatened (7,700 cases), insulted (2,000 cases), or harassed (1,900 cases). Whatever the other reasons were that a teacher felt he or she needed legal advice, we weren't told about them. Added to that, half a million teachers had taken out additional insurance to cover them against the after-effects of accidents or moral or psychological violence.

'Only the *Figaro* could come up with this sort of stuff,' I'd said pointing to the article.

The *Figaro* has belonged to the arms manufacturer and centre-right politician Serge Dassault since 2004, and he has launched numerous campaigns sympathetic to fellow UMP politician Sarkozy; negligent judges and failures of integration were forever cropping up in his reports.

'Why? Because the mistreatment of teachers is a "right-wing" topic?' my acquaintance had asked, bemused.

'Well, it's obvious that the kids are from migrant backgrounds and live in the banlieues.'

'Where does it say that?' he asked and turned to look at me.

And indeed, nowhere in the article did it say, or even suggest, that these teachers were working in the banlieues. I tell this story to underline just how ideologically charged any discussion of schools is in France. The high percentage of students dropping out of school bears witness to the fact that many students from the critical neighbourhoods deem school to be pointless. And even I could not close my eyes to the fact that a young person who had not been through the integration mill of the schools, could quite possibly never be an exemplary French citizen, if only because he would not stand a chance of getting a job. There were in fact certain young French people who did not want to be brought to heel, who had no intention of doing anything which might contribute to the wellbeing of society in general, who didn't give a stuff about society. Some of them fell into crime and often they ended up in prison. A few transformed themselves into holy warriors and devoted themselves to terrorism.

Nevertheless I refused to accept that every report about young people avoiding school in the banlieues inevitably concluded by asking whether these young people were really French. Or French enough to satisfy those who took it upon themselves to decide which social and cultural skills a person needed to adopt in order to be classified as a compatriot, despite the fact that these young people had French passports and were *ipso facto* officially French. Nobody was questioning that the French invented savoir-vivre and beaujolais nouveau, love and the Eiffel Tower, Paris cafés and red and white checked tablecloths in the bistros all French confirmed by the large numbers of American tourists.

But what about révolte, was that French? Was truancy a French phenomenon? And what about violence and criminality? And, since we're asking, given that there are five million Muslims living in France, was a mosque French? Was a synagogue French? Was a synagogue more French than a mosque, or a mosque more French than a synagogue? Was couscous as French as coq au vin?

You can go on asking these questions ad infinitum. And the Front National did go on asking them ad infinitum and ad absurdum; for example when a mayor from a far-right party insists on serving pork in the school canteens in his town because his schools are French schools and do not have to conform to halal laws. Of course you do not need to apply halal laws in provincial French towns, but they should not be ignored – out of respect for those of different faiths. Because, until proven otherwise, respect is also part of French culture.

These days you hear many intellectuals of the right warning of a new national identity crisis. They tell horror stories of foreign infiltration by Muslim immigrants and fear for the survival of their values. As they would have it the schools serve perfectly to prove them right and they never tire of pointing out how all the Poles, Italians, Chinese, Vietnamese, Jewish immigrants from eastern Europe, how all these people who flooded into France to get a better life and a future for their children, they all assimilated, all, that is, except those Muslim kids from North Africa and Black Africa, who would rather set fire to a school than attend it.

By creating a ministry for immigration and national identity in 2007, Nicolas Sarkozy linked the two themes and caused a shudder of horror in left-wing circles, the mere mention of the subject of national identity is interpreted as a way of excluding and stigmatising Muslim citizens and immigrants by sleight of hand. That changed radically after the attacks in 2015, because even left-wing politicians have taken owner-ship of republican emblems, they respond to attrocities by singing the Marseillaise and get misty-eyed before the tricolore flags hanging from many a Paris balcony.

I eventually got an answer to the question of whether terrorism is French; one morning recently I was in my kitchen drinking coffee and listening to an RTL interview with the Home Secretary Bernard Cazenove to mark one year since the *Charlie Hebdo* attack. 'Since 2013 we have broken up eighteen terrorist cells and recruiting channels throughout France, including in Nîmes, Orléans and Strasbourg. We have arrested members of eleven terrorist groups who were planning attacks. And since spring 2015 we were able to foil six attacks.' It could not be much clearer: whether we like it or not, terrorism is a French phenomenon.

PART FOUR

– Left and Right –

I can still see the 2007 presidential election cam-
paign. Ségolène Royale, the socialist candidate,
put forward her programme to rejuvenate the country
should she win. At the time my son was delivering fly-
ers for her party, and my friends organised meetings.
So I listened rather attentively whenever Madame
Royale spoke about 'participatory democracy'. I liked
her and because I liked her I wanted to understand
properly. 'So how is this citizen participation going to
work?' I asked my son. But since he was, as ever, too
busy to be bothered with his mother for any length
of time and failed to give me a satisfactory answer, I
turned to friends. 'Does she mean to send the voters
to the ballot boxes all the time? Will it function via
clubs and associations? Or institutions? Can anyone
sign up? How are we supposed to participate in every
political decision?' I asked, irritated by the general
lack of response.

'You and your eternal German questions,' said my
son in judgement, and proudly declared that Ségolène
(like so many others he called her by her first name, he
was after all a member of the Young Socialists) was the
Queen of the Opinion Polls with her populist tactics.

Her opponent for the presidency promised

something which, to my mind, made so little sense
that I didn't even try to understand it: 'We have to
have a debate about our national identity. I will not
let France stand undefended against immigrants,'
Nicolas Sarkozy assured us, and went on to win the
election. Sarkozy had declared war not on unemployment or global warming but on the residents of the
banlieues and people in asylum camps. The immigrant
as number one enemy of the state. The danger: that
France would be overrun with foreigners.

Whenever anyone in politics talks about identity
it is always in general terms and always in terms of
loss. Even a seasoned strategist like Marine Le Pen
dances round this subject. Because if she had to flesh
out exactly what she means by French national identity
then some sections of her voters might feel excluded.
Madame Le Pen never said exactly what she meant by
La Grande Nation – occasionally implying what it had
once been, back in the good old glory days – but she
did say what France should *not* be: namely a land of
women in headscarves and men with Muslim beards.
In his work *The Human Consequences* the English
sociologist of Polish-Jewish descent Zygmunt Bauman,
with the cynicism of a desperate man, referring to
refugees, the homeless, asylum seekers, migrants – all
those people who are always conveniently to hand for
politicians of all stripes to blame when things start getting tough – calls them the rejects and waste of globalisation. History has ever shown us that foreigners make

perfect scapegoats. And too, that it is easy to stir up fear amongst people who feel insecure. Bauman says:

These people wander the globe in search of a living and try and settle there where they find such a living. And so they all too easily succumb to expression of their fears fed by the widespread angst that they are being pushed to the margins of society.

The fear of sliding into poverty is not assuaged by talk of impending foreign takeover, but such talk does serve as a distraction. It was for this very purpose that immediately after his election Sarkozy named his Minister for Integration, National Identity and Immigration who was going to be responsible for 'Policy, commemoration and furtherment of citizenship and the principles and values of the republic.' It sounds rather wooden and pompous and I am particularly intrigued by how one is supposed to commemorate and further citizenship. At the end of his period in office Minister Eric Besson was not surprisingly none the wiser. He had nevertheless organised seminars and opinion polls, but was still not prepared to talk about exactly what was meant by this concept of belonging. Just a quick anecdote: Today Besson sits on the supervisory board of the French provider of the worldwide money transfer company PayTop, which enables people, mostly immigrants sending financial help back home, to transfer funds quickly. That too is France.

In France, as in most of Europe, the debate on integration is held in terms of ideology. It splits my family and my circle of friends into a left camp and a right camp, and both stick firmly to their respective positions. If we make the mistake of broaching the topic of integration at table and I try, loving consensus as I do, to negotiate between the fronts, then it ends up sounding like this:

Left-wing friend claims that violence in the banlieues is nothing other than an expression of social anger. Instantly, right-wing friend counters: 'Oh yeah, social anger? And what they're doing to the Jews – that's social anger too I suppose? And when they beat up gays? Social anger? And when they grope women under their skirts? Oh, of course, social anger. You are so deluded.' Whereby the 'you' refers to all left-wing thinkers across the board.

Obviously this is where I intervene. 'More rice anyone?' or I start trying to explain: 'What he really means is that the violent acts carried out by a few young Muslim men.'

'I know exactly what he means,' my other friend cuts me off. 'And any minute now he'll start whittering on about feudal patriarchy and forced marriages and honour killings, and then he'll conclude that Islam is a barrier to integration and incompatible with Western democratic principles.'

'Yeah right, because honour killings are part of our Western democracy, are they?' friend number two is bound to say, and because both have gone alarmingly red in the face I make another attempt at mediation. It strikes me actually that both friends were too quick to dismiss the issue of anti-semitism, but the dinner party is at my house so I don't mention it.

'What he means of course,' I start, referring to my left-wing friend, 'is that there are around 30 million Muslims living in Europe and that you can't just suspect them all . . .'

'Does he deny that there are parallel societies in France which are ruled by Sharia law?'

And, me to his opponent: 'He means that if islamic migrants are to integrate then they must recognise pluralism and secular law . . .'

'No, no, no!' bellows my right-wing friend at my left-wing friend. 'That's not what I mean. I mean that the most important reason for the problems with integration is their refusal to integrate.'

Whereupon my left-wing friend, by now turning nasty, simply says, 'Their refusal? What mysterious "they" is he talking about? But then if I was a lawyer like him and lived in a massive mansion in the 8th arrondissement I would probably witter on about refusal instead of unemployment . . .'

'What he means,' I leap in quickly, 'is that we have to get unemployment and poverty under control if we are to integrate immigrants successfully.' That's a challenge, I think – but decide not to say anything – a real Sisyphean task in a society where unemployment is not a temporary blip but has unfortunately become the norm.

I could go on recounting this discussion right up to the sorbet, but it is actually only significant for one reason: it illustrates how little either side is prepared to move towards the other. For reasons of history.

French Marxists were primarily focussed on class war. So national identity had always been abhorrent to them, because it distracted people from issues which seemed far more important to them, issues of growing worldwide social inequality. The left in France never gave a thought to national identity. And their representatives even accused those who did of making social inequality a matter of destiny. It was the feminists and gender researchers who first looked properly into the relation between identity and gender, but that's just in passing because it opens up a whole new area of discussion.

There are certainly other forces at play which mean that someone like me, born and bred in Germany, is wary of any discussion of identity. It brings back too many memories of overblown nationalism and the *Volk, Blut und Boden* rhetoric of the Nazis, their anti-semitism and its fatal consequences. The national socialist ideologues categorically excluded any concept of class affiliation. *The Peoples's Dictionary* of 1943 defined the community of German people as 'A community of peoples based on bonds of blood, shared destiny and common political beliefs, to which all conflicts of class and status are anathema.' They just linked anti-semitism with any sort of class-sociological analysis. Thus the Jews were not only accused of speculating on the Stock Market and of impurely enriching themselves, but also of 'driving honest German workers to the brink of destruction by their sorcery and dervishing round the golden calf'. The Jew was not only an enemy of the people but a class enemy as well. The nonsense about 'Jewish capital', world conspiracy, Jewish speculators and exploiters who did not only control the markets but were bleeding the world's poor, is still a widely held prejudice amongst the Muslim underdogs in the banlieues, and underpins a virulent antisemitism which does not flinch from rape, torture and murder.

One of the attacks which I felt resembled a ritual killing and devastated the world's Jewry, was the murder by torture of Ilan Halimi, a twenty-three-year-old mobile phone salesman, who on 26 January 2006, about six months after the youth riots, was trapped and abducted by a gang from the Bagneux suburb, in order to hold him ransom. The gang, which called itself The Barbarians, demanded 450,000 euros from his family. When they desperately pleaded that they could not possibly raise such a sum, the gang members retorted that Jews were rich and anyway would stick together. The deluded image of world Jewry was so deeply embedded in their minds that it left no room for any other reality. It did not occur to any of the brutal murderers that a rich Jew would hardly be wasting his time in a suburb like Bagneux selling mobile phones. The gangsters tortured the young man for three weeks in a council house basement. Friends and neighbours came by to watch the show, and not one thought to tell the police. They quoted verses from the Quran as they stabbed Halimi and stubbed out burning cigarettes on him, and in Allah's name they cut off one of his ears and a toe. And then they left him to bleed to death from his wounds.

All the gang members were young, the youngest was just seventeen. Almost all of them were unemployed and children or descendants of immigrants from African states, and were French citizens. Frustrated and brutalised, they had lost their bearings and had been radicalised by radical Islamic literature and its preachers. They were all obsessed with 'the Jews' and humiliated by what they imagined to be their wealth and success. Like the attackers of 2015, these losers of the republic had turned to a movement which not only gave them a new identity and reason to live, but also political and religious legitimacy to turn to violence. This movement had handed the 2015 attackers the justification they needed to despise as decadent the republican values which they held responsible for their exclusion. The fact that Islamic ideology demanded absolute obedience and dictated every detail of their daily lives made it all the more attractive to these young men who had mostly been left to themselves. It freed them from the daily chore of deciding what to do and absolved them from all reponsibility for their actions.

The 2015 attackers saw themselves as avengers of an insulted and persecuted religion, and they were prepared to die for that religion. Whilst we in our secular culture see death as a disagreeable occurrence which one should ideally meet with dignity, and the faithful see it as a painful passage into happiness beyond, fascist fanatics glorify it, as Umberto Eco emphasised in his fourteen characteristics of ur-faschism:

[T]he ur-fascist hero craves heroic death, advertised as the best reward for a heroic life. The Ur-Fascist hero is impatient to die. In his impatience, he more frequently sends other people to death.

I followed the trial in the Ilan Halimi murder closely. I was particularly intrigued by the gang leader, Youssouf Fofana, who the investigators described as a perverted psychopath. Between 2000 and 2003, Fofana had been convicted five times for theft, premeditated violence, robbery, and an attack on a policeman. He told the investigators he had been inspired by American film footage from the torture prison Abu Ghraib. I wondered how it had come about that he had succumbed to the delirium of hate. I had read the statements of this young man whose parents came from the Ivory Coast, and I thought, Here's a young man who has internalised the entire violent history of his nation, with its leitmotiv of slavery and exploitation, cultural expropriation and usurpation, despotism, arbitrariness and humiliation, civil war and corruption and transferred it wholesale to the French suburbs. But how was that possible? And what was to be done with the legacy of colonialism? How could they have made a young mobile telephone salesman responsible for all that misery rather than the real perpetrators: the politicians who, ensconced in their solid villas, at least no longer glorify colonial rule as a tool of civilisation, but nevertheless seize on every opportunity to gain more control over Africa through neo-colonialist policies.

In my novel *The Guilt of Others* I answered this question in the only way I could back then, devastated as I was: 'Why did a Jew have to bear the consequences? Quite simply, because the powerless were easier prey than the powerful.'

'If we believe that we have a single identity from birth to death it is only because we construct a comforting narrative or "story of our Self" about ourselves,' writes Stuart Hall in his work on cultural identity. No one, and certainly no one in this day and age, defines themselves exclusively through their national or religious affiliations, or in terms of their social class. We live in democracies which allow us to invent ourselves. In spite of that, it would be fatal to leave the upper hand in any discussion to those who only drag out identity to exclude others. In Germany too, the right wing in particular focusses on identity in the debate on migrants and refugees. And here too with the aim of calling attention to the dangers of foreign infiltration. Until recently the left preferred to emphasise the economic benefits brought by the migrants. At the very least it might be worth asking whether or not a million or more newly arrived refugees to Germany would be prepared to act as a social back-up for a gradually ageing population. It is equally questionable whether migration and experience of war and mass murder make a person more open and tolerant.

What I'm trying to say here is this: even immigrants have faults, weaknesses, prejudices, strengths, wishes, personal ideas and dreams. The time has come for the political left to stop reducing the refugee narrative to an existential state of flight and sanctuary. If Germany is to learn from France's mistakes, then people of goodwill, and not those who are anyway against foreigners, must take a risk and perceive the new arrivals as individuals with their own backstory and identity.

—

In 2005, when I saw the images of the youth riots, I thought of Kafka's parable *Before the Law*. On the news that evening there were pictures from that day's barricaded streets, burning cars and bins with masked youths throwing stones and molotov cocktails at the riot police, that special unit of the national police, which was giving every bit as good as it got. I watched these scenes of violence every evening in my living room while my husband told the children bedtime stories and I thought of Kafka's parable.

A man from the countryside comes to a doorkeeper and asks to be allowed into the law. The doorkeeper says that he can't let him in at the moment. The man thinks about it and asks if he will be allowed to go in later. 'Possibly,' says the doorkeeper, 'but not now.' And he gives the man a stool and sits him down by the door. The man from the country has not expected such difficulties: he thinks that the law should always be accessible for everyone. The gatekeeper tells him that beyond this gate are other gates with more powerful gatekeepers guarding them. The man from the country repeatedly asks permission to enter but is always refused. He sits there for many years. Just before he dies all his experiences over the long years of waiting crystallise in his mind to a single question: 'Everybody aspires to reach the law, so how come that in all these years no one apart from me has asked to be admitted?' The doorkeeper realises the man is dying and in order to make himself understood to the deaf old man he bellows, 'Nobody else could ask for admittance because this entrance was assigned for you alone. And now I'm going to close it.'

The trigger for these riots which, until the 2015 attacks, were considered the most disastrous outrages in France – the press even spoke of civil war – was the death of two young men in the Paris suburb of Seine-

Saint-Denis. Fleeing from the police, fifteen-year-old Zyed Benna and seventeen-year-old Bouna Traoré had hidden in an electricity transformer station, and were killed by a lethal electric shock. News of their deaths raced through the suburbs. News about mistreatment at the hands of the police had always aroused violence in the suburbs. All too often the state and the political system were reduced in the minds of these young people to just such confrontations.

'You're thinking about it because none of the young men from the cités had appeared before civil institutions, other than in their prescibed and familiar role of delinquent,' my then husband suggested when I told him about how I'd been reminded of Kafka. 'You think they had missed their chance.'

The rioters had never approached the government with concrete demands to improve their conditions. But had they missed their chance – at fifteen and eighteen? No, that was not possible.

'You think that they could have sought admittance into the law, instead of seeing the law as their enemy. The thing is, Gila, they would have been fobbed off just like the man from the countryside.'

'Oh I don't know,' I replied. 'I don't know what it is but there's something else.'

As is always the way with Kafka, there is no single, unambiguous solution. The text maintains its mystery. Kafka's heroes go on failing. Why they fail is as unfathomable to us the readers as it is to the heroes themselves. Kafka's man up from the country never attempts to find out *why* he cannot get into the law, and all he is left with at the end of his life is his solitude. In the same way the rioters never crossed the boundaries of their shanty towns nor the borders of their own frustration. For not one of them had stopped to reflect on his own *conditio humana*. Because if the rioters had thought about the political, social, economic, historical or ethnic circumstances that had brought them to set fire to schools, libraries, town halls, kindergartens, barracks or even just cars, then they would have taken their demands before the law, or rather the political instances of the republic.

Later he suggested that Kafka must have been thinking about Nei'lah, the closing prayer for Yom Kippur.

The next morning I stood before part of our bookshelves I seldom venture to. There they all are, Gershom Scholem, Abraham Joshua Heschel, Adin Steinsaltz, Solomon ibn Gabirol, Martin Buber, Baruch Spinoza, Jacob Taubes, Franz Rosenzweig, the Tanach and the Talmud, waiting for me to discover them; and of course all the Midrash literature, all the commentaries and interpretations of the scripts which cause all those who look into them to lose track of time.

I found a translation of the final prayer of the Day of Atonement, which is intoned aloud on the evening before the conclusion of Yom Kippur, whilst the doors of the Torah cabinet are left open, just before the most solemn and mysterious moment of the service, when the shofar is sounded.

> O keep open for us Your gate of mercy,
> At the time of the closing of the gate,
> Now that the day is waning. The day is passing;
> The sun is setting;
> O let us enter Your gate at last.

I found a new clue in a book I had bought in Pollack's antiquarian bookshop on the King George in Tel-Aviv which listed all the Jewish references in Kafka's work. The author refers to the *Pesikta Rabbati 20*, a parable which embroiders on the story of God's appearing on Mount Sinai. In the parable, as Moses is climbing the mountain to get the ten commandments, he comes before the angel Chamuel, the doorkeeper to heaven.

'What are you doing here, O son of Abraham, in this place which belongs to the angels of fire?' Chamuel asks him, and Moses replies, 'I come with the permission of the Highest [. . .], in order to receive the Torah and carry it down to Israel.' And as Chamuel refuses to let him enter he pushes him aside and gets through to an even more daunting watchman, the angel Hadarniel. He gets past him too and finally reaches the Law.

According to Jewish understanding of history, Moses has two functions, each as important as the other. He is the one who brings the law to the people and the one who leads the people out of Egypt. He is thus seen both as a law-giver and a liberator. The story of the exodus of the people of Israel from Egypt is one of the liberation stories that have so marked Western thinking that it is continually being held up as an examplary narrative by revolutionary movements, as Michael Walzer relates in his wonderful book *Exodus and Revolution.*

Liberation theologists in South America were inspired by the exodus from Egypt as were the civil rights movements in the United States. Martin Luther King took it as inspiration for the March on Washington, and its influence can be seen behind the Salt March of a certain Mahatma Ghandi, which ultimately achieved India's independence from Great Britain.

Walzer writes, 'Neither exodus or revolution would be possible without the new ideas of oppression and corruption, or a sense of injustice, or moral abhorrence' and goes on to show how fighters for civil rights, trade unions or movements for reform have told and retold this story of revolt, unique in the history of mankind, and have replayed it in their own centuries-old struggles against social, political or racist oppression.

The retellings which move me the most are the negro spirituals which use the exodus story to condemn segregation and slavery. The songs, when they were sung in churches allowed Afro-Americans to give vent to their zeal. The white masters could forbid them from holding political meetings but could hardly prevent them from quoting the bible. Anyone who has heard a gospel singer strike up the first verse of *Go Down Moses* knows what I mean.

> When Israel was in Egypt's land:
> Let my people go,
> Oppress'd so hard they could not stand,
> Let my people go.
> Go down, Moses,
> Way down in Egypt's land,
> Tell old Pharaoh,
> Let my people go.

In fact Kafka also engaged with Moses but in his own inimitable way. He tried to work out why the prophet chosen by God to lead the people of Israel out of Egyptian slavery into the land of Canaan stops just before he got there. Moses died at 120 on Mount Nebo having espied the land on the far bank of the Jordan. His people make it to the promised land without him. Kafka, writing in his diary, comments, 'Moses did not make it to Canaan not because his life was too short but because it was a human life.' Moses was fated not to see his dream become reality, a fate shared by many a murdered civil rights or peace activist. I would like to remember one in particular who is very important to me, President of Israel Yitzak Rabin who was shot by a Jewish fundamentalist at a peace declaration in Tel-Aviv on 4th November 1995.

—

Neither Kafka's man from the country nor the young firebrand in 2005 had had the advantage of having a man or a movement standing with them to open the gates to the law and lead them out into civil society. Let me be clear: the circumstance that not one of the young people of immigrant background from the French suburbs brought a single political demand either in 2005 or thereafter, must be attributed to the total failure of those parties who had been grandstanding about the fight against social inequality. Where were the unions? Where were the social activists? Where was the whole of the left wing – starting with the social democrats in the Parti Socialiste right through to the Trotskyists in the Ligue Communiste Révolutionnaire? Where were the antiglobalisation critics from the Lutte Ouvrière and the LCR? Where were all those people who talked of a social market economy, of a classless society and of social equality and freedom? One thing's for sure – they weren't in the banlieues.

The underdogs had been expressing their frustration by rioting for thirty years. Thirty years the same tragedy, the same rage, the same explosions of violence and the same political apathy afterwards. How come no party had managed to get them on board? The answer saddens me. Neither the socialists nor the conservatives who have been taking turns in power for decades, have ever managed to see these immigrant kids as anything other than a burden they were obliged to bear. Nobody denied that every now and then one of them managed to climb the social ladder, that there were some rags to riches stories to be told and that some of them were in work and some self-employed. But in the final analysis immigrant children were seen as an insoluble problem. The same series of events played out over and over again: violent outbursts at regular intervals, followed by new policy strategies against poverty and exclusion, also at regular intervals, which were then criticised – at regular intervals.

Right-wing extremists were scaremongering about foreigners taking over, whilst the left remained stuck in its old rhetoric. What hurts me the most, as the grand-daughter of a communist and founder of a kibbutz, is the extent to which the radical left has lost touch with reality. You only need to look at their disastrous election results to see that they are no longer a force for change. Either because they have failed to renew themselves, or because they were incapable of perceiv-ing realities such as the true needs of the underdogs. Either way none of these movements had managed to include immigrant youth into the class war. If you judge on whether there is a greater degree of equality, soli-darity or integration, then it is clear that organisations such as SOS Racism, founded in 1984 and close to the socialist party, or Indigènes de la République to name but two, have failed miserably. Anyone whose daily life is defined by poverty, joblessness and exclusion needs to hear a promise that there is a better world for him out there. Not one of France's political movements has been able to make that promise to the banlieuesards with any credibility, let alone make good on it.

Their low election turnout rates show how little faith the banlieuesards have in political systems: in the département elections in March 2015, 60.2 per cent of the population in Clichy-sous-Bois did not turn out to vote, in Sarcelles 58.2 per cent, in Mureaux 57.3 per cent. Voters only turned out in those towns where the mayor had actually done something concrete in social policy terms. The turnout rate is falling in France year by year. Back in 2010, a journalist writing in *Le Monde* warned that the high numbers of voters not voting (at the time it was in Clichy-sous-Bois and the number in question was 31.3 per cent – dizzyingly high figures by today's standards), represented a worrying phenom-enon, and begged the question, Can any national party claim legitimacy in the light of such low election participation rates? The basis of any functioning de-mocracy is the inclusion of its citizens in the decision-making process. But when the 'people' who everybody is talking about all the time cannot even be bothered to go and vote for or against a party's vision for the future, well then . . .

Increasing numbers of French people limit their right of co-determination to choosing between two strong men or one strong man and a strong woman in the presidential elections every five years. They do not actually believe what the politicians promise in their election campaigns and have not done so for ages. If anything convinces them, it is when not one of the ideas put to them by the candidates on television promises to measurably change their lives. The dogs bark, the caravan moves on.

The low rate of voter participation is one of many signs that French democracy is in crisis. The spectacular rise of Marine Le Pen is another. In the regional elections at the end of 2015 the extreme right got the most votes. In second place came the coalition of conservative parties led by the former Republican president Nicolas Sarkozy. The socialists, the governing party of President Hollande scraped into third place.

'The people have expressed their will with heads held high,' said Marine Le Pen to her cheering supporters at the post-election press conference when the results had been announced. 'This election confirms what official commentators refuse to accept, that our national movement is without a shadow of a doubt the strongest force in France.' Unlike the German Pegida party, according to opinion polls, Marine Le Pen takes her greatest support from young voters. It is the eighteen to twenty-four-year-olds who helped her to victory. And like all populists Marine Le Pen divides the world into Good and Evil. Her enemy has long since ceased to be the evil foreigner, it is now above all the Establishment.

This makes her so much stronger than a Sarkozy. He can always appropriate her anti-foreigner and anti-Islam rhetoric, but he cannot rage against the elite.

His holidays on the yacht belonging to the billionaire Bolloré will not be easily forgotten, nor all the rich beautiful people with whom he and his wife like to surround themselves. Sarkozy can say what he likes but a man of the people he is not.

Marine Le Pen likes to speak to *those at the bottom* about *them at the top*. She denounces the all-devouring monster of Brussels and the political system she is part of and that boosts her poll ratings. Nobody denies that there is a political class in Paris cut off from real life in the rest of the country, but Marine Le Pen manages to make political capital out of it like no one else can. Her programme overlaps remarkably frequently with that of the radical leftist populist Jean-Luc Mélenchon. They both call for France to leave the Eurozone. Both blame Germany for the EU debt crisis. Both demand that relations with Russia be normalised. What distinguishes her from him, in fact from all French politicians, is how quickly she grasps what's going on in the street, what people are afraid of, what moves them and what they yearn for. Marine Le Pen does not only stoke fears, she listens to them, she seeks them out and politicians from all the democratic parties would do well to listen carefully when she speaks and ask themselves why she alone manages to reach the young generation today.

On the tenth day of the 2005 riots, President Chirac turned to the nation on television, after he had solemnly announced the measures the government was going to introduce to regain control over the riots in the suburbs, he talked of a 'crisis of purpose, direction and identity'. Young people had set fire to their neighbours' cars in their own streets, had set their own schools and gymnasiums ablaze, driven by 'a deep unease'. He warned that violence was not the solution, and announced the extension of the state of emergency, which he said was necessary to reestablish order. Then he spoke of exclusion, disadvantage and the daily racism which these young people faced. He said there were neighbourhoods where drug trafficking and violence were part of daily life. Which were marked by unemployment. Where people had to live in rotting buildings. Where children left school and had no prospects once they had dropped out. Where even those who had got qualifications found no job because they had a wrong sounding name and the wrong address. Chirac promised the disadvantaged youth to solve unemployment and appealed to all parties to represent these marginalised people better. He concluded by saying, 'We can build nothing enduring if we do not have respect, we can build nothing enduring if we fight amongst ourselves, we can build nothing enduring unless we combat the poison of discrimination. We can build nothing enduring unless we acknowledge and accept our differences. They are written into our history, they constitute our wealth.'

The next day the whole body politic reacted as expected across the board. The party of government praised the words of courage. The left denounced the state of emergency. The Communists and Greens even said they would fight it. Other parties promised demonstrations in Paris. But hardly any of them referred to the social aspect of the President's speech. Jean-Marie Le Pen, the then leader of the Front National, ranted against immigration as usual and reminded everybody that he had said years ago that the banlieues would burn one day. In his speech Chirac had addressed the troublemakers. They too, he had confirmed, were 'sons and daughters of the republic'. In these very simple yet very symbolic terms he reiterated his belief that the children of the banlieues were not so much questioning the state's efforts to encourage integration when they ran amok, as they were calling on politicians to make good on their integration promises. 'Chirac's kids,' quipped Le Pen at the time, were no more than 'social atom bombs'. The right-wing populist could have had no idea at the time how right he was and that young Frenchmen from Arab immigrant backgrounds who had grown up in the suburbs of Brussels and Paris would blow themselves up in Paris. Almost all the terrorists had spent several months in Syria learning their craft. Political commentators and terrorism experts were unanimous that these well-trained Syrian fighters, completely indoctrinated and hardened by war had finally brought the war to Europe.

PART FIVE

– 13 November 2015 –

'I don't want any link to be made between this working-class neighbourhood and terrorism,' insisted Claude Bartolone, chairman of the Seine-Saint-Denis council and of the National Assembly in an interview that morning on Europe 1, as 110 elite troops from the riot brigade RAID besieged the hide-out of the 13 November terrorists in that suburb. 'The terrorists have nothing to do with the people here, who just want to get on with their lives.' Bartolone positioned himself protectively in front of his constituents: anxious and frightened Muslims, who had felt for a year now that they always had to justify themselves.

Obviously not every resident of the troubled suburbs travels to the Middle East to join the terrorist militia IS. Nor do all French jihadists who go to Syria come from the banlieues. In an interview in the *Mitteldeutsche Zeitung* Peter Neumann, political scientist and founding director of the International Centre for the Study of Radicalisation at King's College London, describes Western jihadists, the European fighters who travel to Syria or Iraq and are blown to pieces as cannonfodder, in the following terms:

There are some who go to Syria to support their Sunni brothers and sisters in the fight against the Assad regime. Then there are others who believe the 'Islamic State' is a jihadist utopia, who want to live there and have children there. And finally others who failed to make it in Western society. Disengaged and without direction, they fall prey to radical Salafist movements who give them rules, structures and a community, everything which they had not known in their lives thus far.

The self-proclaimed warriers of god who had a seven-hour running battle with the police in Seine-Saint-Denis no longer considered themselves to be 'sons and daughters of the republic'. It is impossible to say whether they were genuinely subsumed by the idea of jihadist utopia or whether they just used it to justify their violence. But we do know that they had been lured by the promises of salvation from so-called IS and believed they had found a home and an identity in radical Islam for which they were even prepared to die and to kill.

———

A few hours ago I wrote the following sentences: 'If I could I would go and knock on every door in the French administration to ask the authorities and politicians: Can't you see the potential in these banlieue kids? Are you so smug and unseeing that you don't recognise the strengths within these young people? Do they have to look like you for you to be able to accept them?'

If I could I would introduce quotas for banlieue-sards in political parties and administrations. I would refer them to Giuseppe Tomasi di Lampedusa's novel *The Leopard* and quote what Tancredi replies to his uncle the Prince of Salina when he asks him why he, a noble, had joined Garibaldi's insurrection: 'If we want everything to stay the same, everything must change.'

I am convinced that if the children of those men from Mali, Chad, Camaroon, Algeria, Morocco, the Congo, the Ivory Coast, Gabon, Benin, Burkino Faso, Burundi and Tchibouti who came to France to work on the conveyor belts at Renault or Peugeot, if their children were sitting in the corridors of power now they would be doing things very differently. If some of the African banlieue kids who had often experienced first hand the crimes of despotic potentates had become French diplomats, they would certainly not support a policy dating back to the time of the de Gaulles presidency. Under the banner 'Françafrique' this did all in its power, from falsifying election results to attempted coups to help 'friendly' regimes into power, to ensure France's economic and political hegemony in the countries of their former colonies. If they were at the ministries of the interior and foreign affairs and could take part in the decisions on social policy, war and peace, then France would still be a Grande Nation.

So, a few hours ago it still seemed important to me to respond to Chirac's appeal to the parties to recruit more kids from the banlieues. I thought I had to explain that it was mostly graduates from the elite Grandes Ecoles who held the reins of power, and the idea of training people who had reached the top through their own gifts rather than by wealth or birth had seemed more relevant just five years earlier. In 1950, 29 per cent of the students at these elite schools had been working class. Today it is barely 9 per cent. Just a couple of months ago I'd had a look at the admissions list for ENA (Ecole Nationale d'Administration): of the 3,000 applicants who do the two-year preparatory course to take the tough entrance exam, only 120 pass. This year had no student from the banlieues. To anyone who reckons this is derisory, let me just mention a few of the graduates: François Hollande, Jacques Chirac and Valéry Giscard d'Estaing went there, as did former prime ministers Edouard Balladur, Michel Rocard, Lionel Jospin, Laurent Fabius, Dominique de Villepin and Alain Juppé.

I have not got enough space to print the list of ministers, MPs, senators and euro-ministers. In the private sector the bosses of Airbus, Accor, Axa, EADS, BNP Paribas, RATP, Capgemini, Gaz de France, Lafarge, Peugeot, Vallourec, Société Générale, Fnac, SNCF all went to ENA and know top politicians, ambassadors, bank directors, influential journalists and members of the constitutional council from their student days. The elite in France has been self-generating for too long. For decades the country has been governed by less than 10 per cent of the overall population. How can things possibly be expected to work when these apparently gifted folk occupy the most important posts in the country and the apparently ungifted have the feeling they are being left behind. When we hear again and again that the old school tie network divides up power amongst its members. I meant to talk about the resentment felt by the poor people, about the feeling that France is divided into those who are In and those who stand Outside, into Paris and the rest, into winners and losers. How can things possibly work when virtually a whole nation feels like it's standing on the outside? That's what I wanted to ask.

But then I read that on New Year's Eve in Cologne, 1,000 young men had ganged up together on the square in front of the main station and had committed serious sexual crimes and muggings, that almost all of the victims of these crimes had been women, and off I went again collecting all the news I could find. I read that the perpetrators had been a 'large group of foreigners', 'men from immigrant backgrounds who looked as though they came from north Africa or the Arab countries'. I read about 'chaotic conditions', about 'shocked, weeping girls and women' who had sought protection with the police from 'running the gauntlet through crowds of drunk men' and I was shocked. And of course I also felt betrayed. Ever since September when the first images of the thousands of refugees arriving in Germany had been broadcast in France I, as a

German living in France, had found myself having to justify Germany's asylum policy.

'When she says, "We can do this" who does she mean by "we"? The Germans? The French? The Europeans? Whatever, she doesn't mean me,' said several of my friends. And others said, 'You'll see. Your Angela will bring all the chaos from Libya, Syria and Iraq to your front door.'

'If by chaos you mean refugees –' was often my only reply. Because since September I had been responding to people who said that such a vast influx of young Muslim men brought danger with it (the more moderate of my friends spoke of 'a great challenge'). I had said that you couldn't define people by their ethnicity or gender. And now this. You sit there like an idiot ceaselessly trying to fathom the political and social conditions which make terrorism possible. You sit writing about force of circumstance, poverty, exclusion, indoctrination and brutalisation, and you try to stack up facts to counter the stigmatisation of individuals, and four hours away by train, young Muslim men have nothing better to do than to treat women as objects of their lust, their resentment, their disgust and their frustration.

Tomorrow they'll ring me again, the ones who start their sentences 'I'm really not a fan of Marine Le Pen, but . . .' 'One is really not a fan of Le Pen, but Islam and the French republic really cannot be reconciled. Muslims had a problem with integration, a problem with women, a problem with freedom of expression, with humour, with the West in general, with Europe, with freedom.'

My answer is always the same: 'Right, and how many Muslims do you know which allows you to make sweeping judgements about five million people of that faith living here in France? Do you know more than four, ten, twenty? And the ones you do know, are they like Amedy Coulibaly, or like Mohamed Merah or the Kouachi brothers? Are they violent? Do they have a problem with freedom of expression? Or with the West? Or with Europe? Must we really declare all Muslims to be our enemies because a few of them have declared us to be their enemies? Should we be allowed to define them by their religious community? Or in fact by an extremist faction of that religion, which preaches terrorism? Why are they suddenly not allowed to be anything except Muslims – and that in the land of freedom?'

Damn, I thought, terrible timing. Now you can say what you like, dozens of migrants threatening, groping, robbing and insulting women – that's not so much going to trigger arguments as stifle them. For one thing, now that we have all seen the pictures and heard the reports, it is once again going to be impossible to talk to each other with any degree of objectivity or without bringing ideology into it. Personally I remembered all the reports I had read throughout my life. I thought of all the women and children raped by Congolese and

Rwandan rebels between 2010 and 2013, even though the UN peacekeepers were stationed only a few kilometres away. I thought about the girls and women regularly abused in public during the civil war in Sierra Leone, about the mass rapes in Bosnia, Egypt, India and, of course, I thought about the women who were being abducted, abused and sold as sex slaves by the terrorist militia Islamic State. Sometimes men rape women as part of some geostrategic masterplan, not infrequently in order to harm an entire ethnic or religious group. They convince themselves that they are satisfying their victims' sexual needs. Yet violence against women, even when drunk men 'just' grope women in a crowd, never has anything to do with sexuality, only ever with power and the abuse of power.

I thought long and hard about why I got so angry at the comments made by Henriette Rekers at the press conference on 5 January, almost as angry as at the events themselves. 'There is no suggestion that we are dealing here with people who have settled in Cologne as refugees,' she had said, and in case anyone had any doubts she added that she held 'any such suggestion to be completely unreliable'. Perhaps I had identified with the victims. Perhaps I had felt betrayed on their behalf. Very probably I had hoped that as a woman and as a mayor she would have protected them. Her duty should have been to turn to them and at the very least, mention the devastation caused to so many women. Yet she did nothing of the sort. Instead she wondered how

this 'affront' would be interpreted, what the reaction
would be. The right-wing populist and Eurosceptic
political party AfD, milked it for all it was worth. A
blonde German woman, sexually molested by a dark-
skinned foreigner – their perfect storm – they exploited
it straight away as agit-prop against 'Merkel's refugee
policy'. I would have welcomed it if Frau Reker had
faced up to reality. Mainly because German civilisation is more mature than she thinks it is, and discussion, even heated discussion, is part and parcel of it.
The Mayoress of Cologne reminded me a bit of one of
those mothers of which literature is full, who urge their
daughters not to take things so seriously, don't make a
fuss, it really doesn't matter if Papa's business friend
(such a nice, influential man) touches you a bit lewdly,
it really is best for everybody if nothing is said. It is
the good old-fashioned middle-class double standard,
I thought, and remembered what Ingeborg Bachmann
wrote about Vienna. 'City without integrity,' she had
called the Austrian capital. 'Never a harsh word in the
antechambers, only a hurtful one.'

Many were outraged at the advice Frau Reker
felt obliged to give women. Ideally, they should stay
at arm's length from strangers, she said. Another of
her comments at that press conference on 5 January
finally exposed the nerve. 'We have thought about
this this morning and we maybe should explain to
people from other cultures what our carnival is all
about and the warmth and openness which go with

it, so they don't automatically take this behaviour as an invitation.'

So that means explaining to men that they're not allowed to grope women during carnival? Did she honestly think that the mass assaults on women on New Year's Eve arose from a glitch in communication? Did she really assume that men who touch up women against their will, rip their clothes and underwear, surround them, insult and rob them can be reached by a leaflet on how to behave around women? Even had Reker just descibed the actual state of affairs, as precisely as possible, no more, no less, she would quite possibly never have played down the events to such an extent.

Reker's advice reminded me of what the chairman of the Jewish Council in Germany, Josef Schuster, said to his co-religionists. Given that the number of anti-semitic crimes had risen dramatically in 2014 he wondered 'whether it was really sensible to announce oneself as a Jew by wearing the kippa in problem neighbourhoods, i.e. neighbourhoods with a lot of Muslims, perhaps it would be better to wear a different sort of hat.'

Advising women and Jews on how best to deal with misogyny or anti-semitism implies, crucially, one thing in particular: that it is up to women and Jews to solve the problems of misogyny and anti-semitism themselves. That in fact misogyny and anti-semitism do not have to be tackled by society as a whole and

WE ARE NOT AFRAID

prosecuted as crimes. There is no etiquette guide for victims. Nor for perpetrators. But happily we have the law.

In France, assaults on so-called marginal groups were not seen for what they were either, namely assaults on civil society as a whole. I have often heard Jewish friends say how excluded and alone they felt. They were attacked because they were Jews and they were defended as Jews. A year after the attack on the Jewish Hyper-Kosher supermarket in Paris, the prime minister Manuel Valls commemorated the victims and said 'France would not be France without French Jews.'

Jews were granted citizenship here in 1791. They became citoyens and in return renounced their status as a community. Jews here are as French as German women are German. What do I mean by that? Social enlightenment has failed when people who, for whatever reason, are considered outsiders and are denied equality. Freedom, equality and brotherhood hold for men and women, not just men; for Christians, Jews and Muslims, not just Christians; for heteros, gays, lesbians, trans and queers, not just for the straights. In a country where women, Jews, gays, journalists, librarians, refugees and Muslims are attacked, should we not militate just for women's equality, just for religious and press freedom, just for the culture and right to love who we want, but surely also for our basic laws? Each incident, whatever the scale, is a microcosm of the whole. It may be *just* a woman being groped under her skirt but actually it encompasses all of society.

In the night of 13 November I had rung my old acquaintance. I thought she must be frightened. I woke her up.

'What's the matter?' she asked me.

I replied, 'I'm not quite sure, but they're shooting everybody. They're going through the streets shooting people.' I told her I had to hang up because I needed to find out where the rest of my clan was. Like the rest of us, I spent most of the night reassuring myself that my friends and their children were safe and sound.

I rang my old friend back the next morning. 'Oh it's so awful,' I stammered.

'Yes,' she said. 'It's awful, we're all Jews now.'

—

I've been asking myself a lot of questions recently and not finding any answers. How can we combat the misogynist, homophobic and anti-semitic mindset being disseminated in some parts of the Muslim world without immediately putting millions of people under suspicion who belong to that religion? Is it by excluding them that we create the fertile ground for the radicalisation of young Muslims? Or can they manage, in their search for identity, to let themselves be duped by Salafism, Islam and extremism without help from our well-meaning condescension? Hatred does not help anybody. Nor does exclusion. And we should fight it anywhere it raises its ugly head whether or not it encourages the radicalisation of young Muslims. And yet the question begs itself: Why is the most extreme form of Islam of all religions, counter to basic European values, so attractive to young people? What makes them susceptible to this new fascism? To this blind faith in a single absolute truth, to a cult of tradition, to charismatic, seemingly infallible leaders preaching a cult of heroes, which is actually a death cult? What has so confused them that they yearn for the Leader, the personification of the will of the people, who they can become one with and who absolves them of all responsibility for their life? Why do they want to belong to something greater than themselves? What is it that drives a European, who has grown up in a welfare state with laws that further employment and vocational training, and child allowance and child benefit, housing benefit, pensions, healthcare, unemployment benefit, what drives this man to blow himself up on the 13 November and leave this message claiming responsibility on behalf of the IS terrorist militia:

In a holy attack, enabled by Allah, a group of the faithful, soldiers of the caliphate, Allah granted them strength and victory, targeted the capital of depravity and perversion, the capital which carries the banner of the cross in Europe, Paris. A group which has freed itself from earthly concerns has attacked the enemy, has sought death in Allah's path, has helped his religion, his prophet and his believers, and thus humiliated his enemies.

Not only Muslims but theologians, Imams, researchers in religion, sociologists, psychologists, terrorism experts, judges, elite troops and state defence will have to work out how to deal with terrorism and the politicisation of Islam, which we can no longer ignore and should under no circumstances underestimate. It has now become a question for the whole of civil society. If we want to come up with efficient answers, nobody can refuse to assume responsibility.

—

Horrorstruck, I watched the images of refugees scrambling over railway lines, motorways, across entire mountain ranges in order to reach Germany. And of course, when Angela Merkel a few days previously at her summer press conference declared 'Fortunately, most of us have not experienced being utterly exhausted on the refugee trail, frightened for our lives or our childrens' lives, or our partner's,' I had to think of my father who had survived several concentration camps and two death marches, and who would certainly have died if the Allies hadn't decided to provide for the ten million displaced persons, to feed and clothe them and give them a roof over their heads. My father possessed nothing when he fled a death march out of Buchenwald and ran into a small wood where he collapsed, and was found by an American soldier and rescued.

Over and over again I watched as tired men, women and children were welcomed at the frontier by volunteers. How they were cared for after days of exertion, were given bottles of water and food, and I thought of him. You don't have to have grown up with tales of flight, war and persecution (or like us with silence) to be grateful for these images. I was grateful. I read about creches in Görlitz, cooking evenings in Dippoldiswalde, welcome dinners in Jena, charity bike rides in Kleve, welcome parties in Olvenstadt, football matches in Gonnesweiler, daytrips in Friedrichshafen, swimming lessons in Burghausen, mentoring in Radolfzell, language courses in Hösbach, weeding sessions in Iserlohn and so on. Sometimes I laughed out loud. How well meaning, how naïve, how clumsy but how brilliant these Germans were.

'Germany is strong. Our refrain as we go into this must be: We have done so much, we can do this!' said Merkel back then in her summer speech. And I thought, If anyone can do it it's these pedantic but brilliant Germans.

Of course the euphoria was followed by disenchantment. From my distant city I only noticed it at first via a couple of news items. Never more than a few lines, they were no longer telling of volunteers offering German lessons. Instead they were about refugees fighting in the food queue, or local politicians pleading that these people be housed separately according to ethnicity after a violent confrontation in a refugee hostel, about a group of Syrians fighting several Afghanis, asylum seekers attacking each other with brooms and frying pans, a fight between an Afghan and an Iraqi at the clothes distribution point which fifty to sixty people joined in with.

'You know what worries me?' I said to a German friend. 'It's that the journalists don't just report the violence in the refugee hostels, they try and explain it or even put it into context.'

'What do you mean?' she asked.

'Look, here for example,' I said and read her the headline on a report about a fight. 'Here the journalist feels it is necessary to say in advance that reports of violent fighting can distort the overall picture and that most asylum seekers in the hostels live peacefully with their fellows.'

'Yes, but that's true,' she said.

'Yes, but in that case he'd be better to write a piece about their living peacefully together. If he is going to write about the fighting he should just report the facts and leave it at that.'

Almost all of the reports emphasised that refugees were traumatised people, that feelings easily ran high when different ethnic and religious groups had to co-exist and that many living in emergency housing were living on their nerves.

'It sounds like special pleading to me,' I said. 'As if they were trying to persuade themselves and the readers. As if they wanted to dispel their own misgivings.'

If only they had not idealised each other, I thought. Or rather, not so much idealised as reduced the other to what they had experienced: on their flight on the one side; to the role of the rescuer on the other. If only it could have ended like in a good Hollywood film with them reaching their destination. Arrival, bottle of water, music and credits. But no, it went on to exhaustion and attrition, and was still going now with all the cultural differences which had emerged, with all the expectations on both sides which were necessarily overtaken by reality.

A warning alarm should really have sounded when I heard Syrians, Albanians and Iraqis all chanting 'Merkel, Merkel' and 'Germany, Germany' from the buses driving through Austria from Hungary to Germany. Frau Merkel as Moses? Germany, the promised land? And when I saw the pictures of reception committees and lines of people applauding the refugees on station platforms, I should have had a premonition of what was coming, but I was merely moved.

The refugee story, or rather the images showing the flight of hundreds of thousands of people, this exodus on foot along country roads, with what little they had in bags or their hands. The tired expressionless faces of the men, women and children, the animosity in the faces of the Hungarian police escorting the line of refugees. The refugees themselves just about hanging in there on the floors of the stations. All these images illustrated the most impressive retelling of the exodus story of recent decades. And the fact that we did retell it and got emotionally involved in the retelling, is a sign not only of our wish for a happy outcome in these difficult, complex and even dangerous times, but also of our utopian longing for brotherhood.

'The world sees Germany as a land of hope and opportunity, and that is far from having always been the case,' said Angela Merkel in her summer address, just before she flung the gates into Germany wide open. The Germans wanted to do good. And they have not failed. I far prefer a Frau Merkel who declares, 'We can do this!' to a Thomas de Maizière who in *Heute-Journal* criticised the behaviour of some refugees. 'It must be said,' declared the Minister for the Interior, 'that Germany expects the refugees to behave like newcomers,' and sounding like a disappointed host, he went on to say that the refugees had been grateful up until the summer, but that things had changed since. I think Merkel's utopian enthusiasm is much braver than the pragmatic objection from former chancellor Schröder, who declared, once the mood in Germany started to swing, that the asylum policy of his successor was 'completely unrealistic', which is what any of us could have said right from the start.

At last politicians of all stripes are calling for harsher laws against criminal immigrants and tighter controls during the registration process of each individual new arrival. At last people are talking about our value system, our basic rights which govern behaviour between citizens and which, if respected, make for peaceful cohabitation. About time.

The *Déclaration des droits de l'homme et du citoyen*, the declaration of the rights of man and citizen, proclaimed on the 26 August in the French national assembly, is based on the thinking of the Enlightenment. I will just mention three articles.

Article 1: Man is born free and equal and remains so.

Article 10: No one shall be persecuted on the basis of his opinions, even of religious nature, as long as their expression does not trouble public order as established by law.

Article 11: The freedom to express thoughts and opinions is one of the most precious human rights: thus any citizen may speak, write and print freely subject to his being responsible for any abuse of that freedom in the cases set out in law.

I would also like to mention the first article of the 'Declaration of the Rights of Woman and the Female Citizen' which the womens' rights activist Olympe de Gouges brought before the national assembly in 1791: *Woman is born free and remains equal in rights to man.*

And as well I want to refer to article 3 of the German constitution which was proclaimed at a public meeting in Bonn in 1949. There it says (1) *All people are equal before the law* and (2) *Men and women are equal. The state shall require this equality to be enforced and shall work to remove any existing discrimination.*

The violent excesses of New Year's Eve have rung in a new refugee policy in Germany. Even before the Cologne attacks, Sweden had reintroduced border controls, Norway and Denmark had decided to tighten their asylum laws, Hungary was building fences, Austria was considering 'plans for special building measures' on the border with Slovenia. Slovenia itself had started work on a fence along its border with Croatia. But in Germany, anyone, like Josef Schuster, chairman of the central Jewish council, who suggested that the country's capacity to welcome, care for and integrate refugees was finite, was shouted down. Schuster called for more controls at the point of entry. Specifically, in an interview in *Welt* in November 2015, Schuster said, 'Many of the refugees are fleeing IS terrorism and want to live in peace and freedom, but at the same time they come from cultures imbued with anti-semitism and intolerance. This is not just about the Jews. It is about equality between men and women, about the treatment of homosexuals.'

Not a happy turn of phrase to be sure, but the upsurge of fury that ensued from this comment looks strange seen from today's perspective. Back in November, Schuster was accused of racism and it was suggested that the central council of Jews should call itself the 'central council of racist Jews'. Yet a mere two months later, former Chancellor Schröder brought 'healthy German good sense' into the mix: 'Such people have no place in Germany,' he said, referring to the New Year's Eve rowdies. And no one suggested he should be called 'the former Chancellor of racist Germans'.

—

'Because the world is built by mortals, it wears out.'
This sentence, which could have been written by
Kafka, comes from a lecture given by Hannah Arendt
in 1958 in Bremen. But unlike with Kafka, here not
only is the failure itself specified but the mechanism
behind it. Hannah Arendt dedicated her lecture to her
friend Erwin Loewenson on his seventieth birthday.
The lecture deals with the crisis in education. I had
got this lecture out again having read it as a student in
Jerusalem, after I had seen Chirac's television speech
on the riots in the banlieues. I had been struck by
something he said.

'Children and young people need direction and
values,' he had said. 'Parental authority is crucial to
conveying these. Families have to assume their responsibilities. If they abdicate these responsibilities, then
we will punish them according to the law.'

Was the crisis of identity and direction that Chirac
had talked about really nothing other than a crisis of
education? Had parents failed? I remembered that
Hannah Arendt in that speech had referred to the crisis in education as one aspect of a general crisis which
she, in the early Sixties, felt was affecting the whole
world and virtually all areas of human life. I hoped I
would perhaps find some food for thought here, looked
out the lecture and rang my friend who is a lawyer.

'Were any of the rioters' parents prosecuted during the youth riots?' I asked.

'How do you mean?'

'Were parents taken to court because they had failed in their duty of care?'

She rephrased my question in lawyerly terms: 'You mean, were they sued for damages as a result of failure of duty of care?' She paused, then: 'Gila, we're not talking about seven-year-olds who got up to mischief when Mum left them alone in the garden for ten minutes. They burned down schools, sports halls.'

'No, no,' I interrupted. 'Not sued for damages.'

'What for then?'

I told her about Chirac's speech and she laughed. 'That was just something he said to reassure his right-wing electorate.'

I retorted that she was wrong. This wasn't the politician speaking but the President. I wasn't able to explain more clearly. I had watched the speech twice, Chirac wearing glasses for the first time, and something about the tone and the choice of words, the way he looked into the camera, something I couldn't quite put my finger on, had made me feel, ten years later, that not only was he aware of the importance of what he was saying but also that he must have known it would achieve nothing.

'He was bluffing,' I suggested. 'He obviously knew he didn't have anything against the parents of the rioters. He bluffed to shake them up.'

'How are you supposed to control a young person who has run completely wild? You're kidding yourself,' my friend said.

117

'No, he didn't want them to control them but to educate them.'

Hannah Arendt in her lecture, which now, thirty years on, I realised was not a call for authority, which at the time I had felt to be reactionary, defines education as something 'we do basically for a world which has lost or is losing its bearings'. That the world was losing its bearings did not strike Hannah Arendt as an exceptional circumstance, rather as the normal human condition. 'Because the world is built by mortals, it loses its way.' And because it is constantly drifting, we, the mortals, 'must constantly steer it back on course'.

We have become a service-based society, and a bank employee, or a facility manager, or a market researcher, or a call centre agent may well have forgotten – but I think that if you ask a primary school teacher who every year teaches children to read and write, or a doctor, a nurse, midwives, healers, social workers, psychologists, judges, public prosecutors . . . ask any of them, and after a moment's thought they would all agree that every day in their own small way each of them tries to steer the world back on course.

For Hannah Arendt education was nothing other than creating the basis which allows it just to be *possible* to readjust the world's bearings.

I have read a pile of reports and articles on the educational disadvantages of children from migrant backgrounds, on the causes and various attempts at solution, the very words 'migrant background' send

me to sleep. I read all these studies rather half heart-
edly, because I keep being told that integration has to
do with learning and learning to do with education.
I read them because I want to understand terrorism
and because the al-Suris of this world have got their
eyes on young, badly integrated, European Muslims
and converts, because they can get them to carry out
attacks in the heart of our cities in order to kill in-
fidels, like a few concert goers or Jews or presumed
enemies of Islam like the *Charlie Hebdo* cartoonists. I
read them because terrorism is the most radical rejec-
tion of integration.

By now I know quite a bit about this subject. I
could get away with pretending to be an integration
officer at a conference, or at least I could hold forth
convincingly for an hour before the tea and biscuits.
For example, I know that more immigrant children
finish school and go to university in France than in
Germany, where they all-too-soon finish up in vocational colleges. But I also know that in France there
is almost no safety net for those who do not make it. I
know that parenting skills need to be improved.

As I write I think of Mohamed Merah, the attacker
who shot dead seven people over the course of three
days, in the Toulouse area – three French soldiers of
migrant background, three children and the teacher
at a Jewish school. Merah came from an Algerian family who loathed France. For weeks now I have been
reading specialist literature on education, the school

system, reforms, language tests, extra language coaching and every now and then I say to myself, okay, fine, but what, if you please, has all this got to do with preventing terrorism?

It took a thinker like Hannah Arendt to free the word 'education' from the straitjacket of specialist jargon, and make it radical again. In *Die Krise der Erziehung* (The Education Crisis) Arendt differentiates between a teacher's authority and what qualifies him to teach. His qualification consists of his knowing the world he teaches about, his authority lies in his assuming responsibility for that world.

I thought long and hard about who I knew that possessed the authority to teach. My thoughts turned to Latifa Ibn Ziaten who could neither read nor write when she left Morocco at the age of seventeen to join her husband in Rouen, Normandy. Ever since the death of her second son Imad, who had joined the army to become a parachutist, this Muslim woman, complete with headscarf, has been going into schools in the difficult neighbourhoods and talking to young people about her son and his murderer Mohamed Merah. A year after her son's death she told an RMC interviewer why she did it.

I wanted to see where Merah grew up. I went into his neighbourhood and came across a group of young people. We got talking and they told me Merah was a hero and a martyr, and I told them who I was.

Latifa Ibn Ziaten has founded a '*Peace organisation*' and she organises for young people from the banlieues at risk of being indoctrinated to meet 'the enemy' face to face.

My thoughts also turn to Rabbi Michel Serfaty and Imam Mohammed Azizi who drive around the banlieues together in a bus, talking to young people and showing them that it is possible to be friends with people of a different religion. They are often, but by no means always, insulted.

In Arendt's text I found one of the best definitions of society. As she saw it the world was made by 'mortal hands [. . .] in order to house mortals for a limited time'. I find it immensely comforting to think that that every day people nudge the world back on course so that it can go on being our home. That we are only in it for a short time. This was not only an expression of metaphysical perception, but had its roots in Arendt's experience of exile.

– Afterword –

Exactly ten days after the Paris attacks I had a reading in Berlin. I had been invited to this lecture series a good six months earlier. It was called 'Reading Europe' and I had written a brief text about the city of Lemberg which I had recently visited because the protaganist of my new novel came from there. One should actually say Lwiw, because that's the city's current Ukrainian name. One could also use the Russian or Polish names since the city has been kitted out with three complete nationalities, not counting the painful intermezzo of the German occupation. Three times new flags have been raised, whole population groups expelled, memorials torn down, streets renamed, national anthems learned by heart, events in the nation's history reworked. But I had written a text on Lemberg, that place with all its fine houses, its German colonialists, Jewish traders, Polish officials of the Imperial and Royal Hapsburg administration and Ruthenian craftsmen, with its Russian and Armenian streets, its Jewish quarter, its forty-five synagogues and prayer houses, wooden churches and three archbishops. Because like all Jews I mourned the Hapsburg trading metropolis where Poles, Jews, Armenians, Hungarians and Ruthenians had lived, worked and brought up their families alongside each other, in the final act of the Old World, played out in the East of the monarchy, before old Europe became infected with the idea of national and racial purity. On the other hand, the new Europe of rules and regulations that they have cobbled together in Strasburg and Brussels leaves me cold. I don't even know the names of all the members who sit on all the committees and delegations, and who, I sometimes think, have been farmed out to Europe to get rid of them from national or regional politics.

In the summer when I had seen the first images of refugees and followed the media coverage of what was happening to these people pouring across the Balkans or the Mediterranean to get to Europe, I realised that my lecture, which was an attempt to posit a counter model to the rising nationalist and populist movements in Eastern Europe, could not actually grasp the scope of this catastrophe. But then as a novelist was I supposed to be able to reflect everything back aesthetically and process it all with a critical eye?

I read about refugees transported by people smugglers to Greek islands or sheltered (or drowned) in the Mediterranean. I read about daily life in the war and the refugee camps, about appalling conditions particularly for women and children, and about budget cuts at the UN, and fences and border controls with water cannon. And then, people close to me started dying. People in bars and cafés having a drink or a meal with friends, or at a concert or a football match. I wrote to the organiser of the lecture series to say that I couldn't possibly read my original text. That everything happening around me had actually rendered me speechless, and he rang me immediately and asked if I would rather speak about the events in Paris.

At first I thought I couldn't, but the next day I accepted. I wouldn't talk about the attacks and certainly would not waste my breath on the murderers. But instead I wanted to speak about the victims. They had all been young, most of them in their thirties, educated and brought up in a multicultural society. It would have taken ten minutes to read out all their names at the memorial service at the Cours des Invalides.

The next day I sat down at my desk to prepare my lecture. I had decided to open with a quote from Montesquieu: 'It is only when in a strange country that one sees how multicoloured the world is,' he wrote in *Lettres Persanes* and stated that knowing about the many-layered nature of the world was a guarantee that people could co-exist. The victims had come from more than fifty different towns in France and from seventeen countries. They had come from Belgium, Italy, Spain, Portugal, Germany, Great Britain, Sweden, Romania, Morocco, Algeria, Egypt, Burkino Faso, Venezuela, Chile, Mexico, Brazil and the USA and had moved to Paris to study, or to work as programmers and architects, graphic designers, mask makers, sound managers, musicians, tilers, policemen, barmen, pubkeepers and so much more.

President Hollande on the occasion of the memorial: 'We will not give in. We will continue going to stadiums, to listen to music and chansons.'

The appeal not to give in, to go on as before, was heeded by many who celebrated in the days following the attacks. There was nothing solemn about these exuberant and extravagant celebrations. There was more of an urgency about them, as if there was not one minute to be lost before meeting friends and spending the evening with them. It even made some people photograph themselves on a terrace with a glass of wine or a bottle of beer and post them under hashtags like #jesuisenterrasse, #notafraid or #memepaspeur. The quantity of these selfies on Facebook and Twitter allows an insight into the mental state of the Parisians, their need to reassure themselves of their hedonism and lust for life.

'If it goes on like this,' I said to two friends, jokingly complaining about all the parties I'd been invited to since the terrorist attacks, 'then my liver is going to go on strike.'

'Look at it positively,' replied one. 'It's never been so easy to express opposition.'

'Nor so much fun,' added the other.

In an edition of *Charlie Hebdo* which came out right after the attacks, the cartoonists with their usual eye for human absurdity, mocked this attitude. On the cover there is a picture of a man shot through with holes dancing and holding a bottle of champagne.

*They've got guns? We don't give a fuck. We've got cham-
pagne* it says on the front page.

'This is the only answer we should give the terrorists: that their attempt to trigger terrorism is in vain,'
declared the editor-in-chief Riss in his editorial that
week.

Humour is the ability to laugh at oneself, one's
culture, traditions and prejudices. Humour is an ac-
knowledgement that there are other ways of living
and thinking. Humour opens the door wide to others.
'Fanatics can't stand happiness,' said novelist Salman
Rushdie in a recent interview, who had been living
under a Fatwah proclaimed against him by Ayatollah
Khomeini since 1989 because of his masterpiece *The
Satanic Verses.* Apparently the first thing the Taliban
did upon coming to power was to forbid all music and
close cinemas and theatres. That's why humour is a
good antidote to terrorism.

We're so used to sitting in cafés or restaurants, going to concerts or watching football matches that we
have forgotten what the presumption is behind any
kind of socialising, namely mutual respect. Almost
all those who died on 13 November were Parisians by
choice. You can recognise a Parisian not only by how
he talks, where he lives and his manners, but above all
by the fact that he knows how to co-exist with others.
You recognise him by his urbanity. France is a land of
immigrants and Paris a city which requires that its citizens acknowledge and respect each others' differences.

Living in a big city you are faced with other ways of life and different worlds and you learn to deal with them. In a big city you are aware, as Kurt Tucholsky in his poem *Eyes of the City* so brilliantly describes, of 'a pulse beating along foreign veins'.

The metrosociologist Hans Paul Bahrdt defined urban behaviour as the recognition that the other person, however odd his behaviour may be, has an individuality which sees that behaviour as reasonable. And he called the capacity to then respect that individuality with no hope of ever being able to understand it, an 'abdicating humanity'.

The virtue of citizens to consider others as equal is constantly present in Paris. Its citizens rebelled against feudality and took to the streets in the name of liberty, equality and fraternity. And when people from fifty French towns and seventeen different nations were enjoying themselves alongside each other, then they were doing nothing other than taking the Enlightenment idea that we are all equal despite our differences, and celebrating it joyfully and exuberantly.

I had learned quite a bit about the victims because they had completely captured my attention. And I was not alone in wanting to know as much as possible about them. Almost all my friends felt the same. We all felt that we too could have been among the victims, or our partners, children, sisters, brothers, colleagues or neighbours, and all of us indirectly knew someone who had died or been badly injured.

In the first week after the attacks I was sitting opposite a young woman in the underground. She had dyed ash blonde hair, a cherry red mouth and a lovely decolleté and if she hadn't been wearing trainers and green workman's trousers with lots of pockets she could have passed for Jayne Mansfield's younger sister. Everybody in the compartment was watching with embarrassment because she was crying silently as she read *Libération* which had given over its entire edition to the victims. We all knew how she felt. A man proffered her a tissue and she thanked him with a nod.

Day by day, investigators were making new discoveries, and we were getting more and more insight into the terrorist network.

'Did you know that two of the attackers had been able to travel the Balkans route to France on passports registered as stolen?' I asked a friend.

'How can that be possible?' he replied.

'The authorities on the Greek island of Leros failed to check the numbers against the European database,' I said. We moaned a bit about the Greeks, and then moved on to the victims.

I wondered why we always went back to talking about the victims. Was it some sort of catastrophe voyeurism? Were we sensation junkies? No better than the curious onlookers who gather on the pavement to gawp at traffic accidents. Why did hundreds make the pilgrimage every day to the sites of the attacks to leave candles and flowers and page-long poems and texts? I think it was because at least since January 2015, we had been hearing over and over again about the lives of the terrorists, which were always the same. I just did not want to her any more about young men who, instead of finishing school, slid into petty crime. Who, instead of falling in love and moving in with their girlfriends, fell in with the teachings of hate preachers and went off to Syria to learn how to use a Kalashnikov.

Whatever hopes and dreams these young men may have had when they were growing up, once they had turned to terrorism they had become no more than its willing executors.

They had called their victims decadent, had de-humanised them, compared them to vermin who stood in opposition to their vision of life. I do indeed believe we were trying to find a glimmer of human-ity in this catastrophe and found it in the anecdotes and tales which the victims' families, friends and col-leagues shared with us, the countless strangers as we expressed our sympathy.

So as I set off to my lecture in Berlin I had many pages on the lives of those who had died that Friday night in the Le Carillon bar in the Rue Alibert or in the Cambodian restaurant opposite, in the Café Bonne Bière in the Rue du Faubourg-du-Temple, in La Casa Nostra, in the bar La Belle Equipe, in the café Comptoir Voltaire or in the Bataclan theatre.

But as I went up the two steps to the stage, I broke down. I had intended to tell my German audience that

Mathias Dymarski had been studying engineering and had just won his first contract as project manager in a company, that he had made a name for himself in his friendship group as a BMX freestyle rider calling himself 'McCain'. That he had moved to Paris with his girlfriend, Marie, who he'd been in love with since high school in Metz, after an Erasmus year which he had spent in Barcelona and she in London. That their tickets to the Eagles of Death Metal concert had been a birthday present from friends and that Mathias and Marie died aged twenty-two and twenty-three at the sixth song. And I could have told them about Nohemi Gonzalez, one of the nineteen murdered at 21.36. She had grown up in a little town in South California, her parents came from Mexico, and Nohemi was the first of her family to go to university and had wanted to be a designer – and in this context she had spent her exchange year at the design school in Sèvres. I could also have said that Hodda Saadi had invited her friends, her brother Khaled and her sister Halima to the La Belle Equipe café to celebrate her thirty-fifth birthday. Her parents had emigrated from Tunisia and she and her seven siblings had a happy childhood in Saône-et-Loire in Burgundy. Hodda had died immediately. Her sister Halima died of her injuries in the arms of her brother Khaled. I could have told them about Stella Verry's parents who had left Madagascar in order to give their children an education in France: Stella had received a scholarship to study pharmacy but had switched to medicine like her younger sister Vanessa. And I could have told them that the twenty-eight-year-old Salah El-Gebaly who came from a small town in Egypt, was a tiler and lived in a small flat in Val-de-Marne with his cousin Mohamed who was a painter in the same firm. He sent money home regularly and had recently married.

Some papers, particularly the foreign press, highlighted the fact that the terrorists had targeted a given lifestyle. They called their victims 'bobos', who belonged to a sort of bourgeois bohemia, despised by the attackers. It is true, all the victims were employed, many had studied or were still studying and had all travelled at some point in their young lives and were open to other cultures and customs. And it is true too that they had all been enjoying themselves that Friday evening with friends, family or colleagues. They were sitting together, eating, drinking, chatting, making plans, flirting, arguing, laughing, dancing and listening to music. Yet to assume this generation, since named 'generation Bataclan' in the press, had faced no material future worries is to totally ignore the social and economic realities confronting young people even in Europe.

I have read an awful lot of commentaries, anecdotes and elegies written by their families and friends. Not a single one mentioned the attackers or tried to incite hatred. Nobody wrote about the anger, the feeling of powerlessness, the desperation which they must surely have been feeling. Instead, as I've already shown, they reiterated that now, more than ever, was the time to go out and buy your mates a round of drinks. And they recounted the trips, the encounters, the plans of those who died and remembered their quirks and foibles with gently ironic melancholy. Hardly anybody got bogged down in the usual generalisations about good and evil or platitudes about the West and our culture. What counted were the details, all the apparent trivial things which go to make up a life: Julien Galisson's favourite foods were pasta and cornflakes. Anna Pétard Lieffrig collected coins and hats. Thierry Hardouin smoked Havanas. Ludovic Boumbas appreciated good rum, soul, funk and flowers. Elif Dogan moved to Paris 'to eat in at least twenty-five good restaurants and taste fifty-eight different wines'. Hugo Sarrade read mangas, was a fan of the English group Prodigy and on his last trip to the Far East had had two Kanjis, which means freedom, tattooed on the right side of his chest. Marie Mosser could play Chopin's étude op. 19 faultlessly without sheet music.

In the end I said nothing about the victims. I couldn't manage it. Instead I read Arthur Rimbaud's poem *Roman*. I had asked a Cologne bookseller to e-mail me a German translation and he agreed the poem was wonderful and it was a very good idea. I said the poem had been written by someone who had been more able than anyone else to capture the lightness of being of the young, and that I could think of nothing more fitting to commemorate the victims. This is what I read:

You're not serious, when you're seventeen.
– One fine evening, tired of beers and lemonade,
The noisy cafés with their dazzling gleam!
– You walk the lime-trees' green on the Parade.

Back then up on the podium I felt a bit ridiculous, offering a mere poem as a response to terror. This feeling of powerlessness, of not responding appropriately, of not being able to do what seems necessary is something I share with many.

Recently a friend of mine told me of how she had gone up to a young Muslim on the Place de la République. He was standing blindfolded and offering 'free hugs'.

We were sitting in my local, drinking white wine. The bar was emptier than usual, the waiters as rude and inattentive as ever. She had hugged him, she said, and cried a little. 'Pretty embarrassing, isn't it?' she asked.

'Borderline,' I replied.

'We were standing round the young man. About twenty people. And we hugged him and clapped our act of solidarity with our fellow man.'

'Very, very embarrassing,' I said.

But what do I know? The world is drifting well off course at the moment. We shouldn't allow some arbitrary scruple to hold us back from trying to set it back on course again.

Notting Hill Editions

Notting Hill Editions is devoted to the best in essay writing. Our authors, living and dead, cover a broad range of non-fiction, but all display the virtues of brevity, soul and wit.

Our commitment to reinvigorating the essay as a literary form extends to our website, where we host the wonderful Essay Library, a home for the world's most important and enjoyable essays, including the facility to search, save your favourites and add your comments and suggestions.

To discover more, please visit
www.nottinghilleditions.com

Other titles from Notting Hill Editions*

Alchemy: Writers on Truth, Lies and Fiction
Introduced by Iain Sinclair

A collection of essays by Joanna Kavenna, Benjamin Markovits, Gabriel Josipovici, Partou Zia and Anakana Schofield.

Five writers grapple with the reality and fiction, and the alchemical process of turning life into art. They try to explain the impulse to write 'by way of personal anecdote, revelation, or hopeful punt in the dark.'

The Paradoxal Compass: Drake's Dilemma
by Horatio Morpurgo

In this compelling historical narrative and environmental manifesto, Morpurgo compares our own tipping point with the 'great unsettling' faced by the Elizabethans more than four centuries ago. Morpurgo dramatizes the perilous hours during which Drake's *Golden Hinde* was stranded on a reef off the coast of Indonesia, and asks what was really at the heart of Drake's violent quarrel with Fletcher, the ship's chaplain.

Nairn's Paris
by Ian Nairn
Introduced by Andrew Hussey

Last printed in 1968, this is a unique guidebook from the late, great architectural writer Ian Nairn, illustrated with the author's black and white snaps of the city. Here is an idioscyncratic and unpretentious portrait of the 'collective masterpiece' that is Paris.

CLASSIC COLLECTION

The Classic Collection brings together the finest essayists of the past, introduced by contemporary writers.

Drawn from Life – Selected Essays of Michel de Montaigne
Introduced by Tim Parks

Grumbling at Large – Selected Essays of J. B. Priestley
Introduced by Valerie Grove

Beautiful and Impossible Things
– Selected Essays of Oscar Wilde
Introduced by Gyles Brandreth

Words of Fire – Selected Essays of Ahad Ha'am
Introduced by Brian Klug

Essays on the Self – Selected Essays of Virginia Woolf
Introduced by Joanna Kavenna

All That is Worth Remembering
– Selected Essays of William Hazlitt
Introduced by Duncan Wu